PROPERTY OF INDIAN TRAILS
PUBLIC LIBRARY DISTRICT

Stress-Proof Your Life

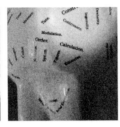

52 Brilliant Ideas

one good idea can change your life

Stress-Proof Your Life

Smart Ways to Relax and Re-Energize

Elisabeth Wilson

A Perigee Book

For Jim. The only man worth getting de-stressed for.

A PERIGEE BOOK
Published by the Penguin Group
Penguin Group (USA) Inc.
375 Hudson Street, New York, New York 10014, USA
Penguin Group (Canada), 90 Eglinton Avenue East, Suite 700, Toronto, Ontario M4P 2Y3, Canada
(a division of Pearson Penguin Canada Inc.)
Penguin Books Ltd., 80 Strand, London WC2R 0RL, England
Penguin Group Ireland, 25 St. Stephen's Green, Dublin 2, Ireland (a division of Penguin Books Ltd.)
Penguin Group (Australia), 250 Camberwell Road, Camberwell, Victoria 3124, Australia
(a division of Pearson Australia Group Pty. Ltd.)
Penguin Books India Pvt. Ltd., 11 Community Centre, Panchsheel Park, New Delhi—110 017, India
Penguin Group (NZ), 67 Apollo Drive, Rosedale, North Shore 0632, New Zealand
(a division of Pearson New Zealand Ltd.)
Penguin Books (South Africa) (Pty.) Ltd., 24 Sturdee Avenue, Rosebank, Johannesburg 2196,
South Africa

Penguin Books Ltd., Registered Offices: 80 Strand, London WC2R 0RL, England

While the author has made every effort to provide accurate telephone numbers and Internet addresses at the time of publication, neither the publisher nor the author assumes any responsibility for errors, or for changes that occur after publication. Further, the publisher does not have any control over and does not assume any responsibility for author or third-party websites or their content.

STRESS-PROOF YOUR LIFE

Copyright © 2005, 2007 by The Infinite Ideas Company Limited
Cover design by Liz Sheehan
Text design by Baseline Arts Ltd., Oxford

All rights reserved.
No part of this book may be reproduced, scanned, or distributed in any printed or electronic form without permission. Please do not participate in or encourag piracy of copyrighted materials in violation of the author's rights. Purchase only authorized editions.
PERIGEE is a registered trademark of Penguin Group (USA) Inc.
The "P" design is a trademark belonging to Penguin Group (USA) Inc.

First American edition: April 2008
Originally published in Great Britain in 2005 by The Infinite Ideas Company Limited.
A second UK edition followed in 2007.

Perigee trade paperback ISBN: 978-0-399-53405-8

PRINTED IN THE UNITED STATES OF AMERICA

10   9   8   7   6   5   4   3   2   1

Most Perigee books are available at special quantity discounts for bulk purchases for sales promotions, premiums, fund-raising, or educational use. Special books, or book excerpts, can also be created to fit specific needs. For details, write: Special Markets, Penguin Group (USA) Inc., 375 Hudson Street, New York, New York 10014.

Brilliant ideas

Brilliant features

Each chapter of this book is designed to provide you with an inspirational idea that you can read quickly and put into practice right away.

Throughout you'll find four features that will help you to get straight to the heart of the idea:

- *Here's an idea for you* Give it a try—right here, right now. Get an idea of how well you're doing so far.

- *Try another idea* If this idea looks like a life-changer then there's no time to lose. *Try another idea* will point you straight to a related tip to enhance and expand on the first.

- *Defining idea* Words of wisdom from masters and mistresses of the art, plus some interesting hangers-on.

- *How did it go?* If at first you do succeed, try to hide your amazement. If, on the other hand, you don't, then this is where you'll find a Q and A that highlights common problems and how to get over them.

Introduction

The Chinese have an old saying, so I'm told: "Stress and madness are twin sisters—they always go hand in hand." For the last couple of decades we've accepted escalating stress levels as the price we pay for "having it all," but now we're waking up to the second half of the equation—the madness part.

"Having it all" translates, as we know, into "doing it all." And as the number of roles we're gleefully supposed to inhabit grows we're "being it all," too. Women are used to hearing how difficult it is to inhabit their multitasking, multi-role lives. But I'd hazard it's the same for men—not only do they have to be exemplary hunter-gatherers (even more so than previous generations), but they are expected to be fabulous fathers, wonderful lovers, and nice to their moms. They used to have wives for that sort of thing, but no longer in the double-income family of the twenty-first century.

So we know stress is A Bad Thing. It leeches our energy and is the forerunner of just about every major illness around, and quite a few minor ones, too. And we know that the ability to relax is A Good Thing, but since you can't get it in pill form from your pharmacist and have to do it yourself, the relaxation thing causes quite a few problems for us, too. It's yet another thing to add to the to-do list.

This book was written with my friend, Rosalind, in mind. She once said to me, "Wouldn't it be marvelous if brushing our teeth was as good as meditation?" This was after she had given up her brand-new hobby of listening to a relaxation tape, morning and evening, after just four days. Well, to be honest three and a half because she was too exhausted to do it on the fourth evening.

This book is for people like her who are super-busy and for whom the usual advice doesn't apply. Let's face it, if you're the sort of person who enjoys doing an hour of yoga every morning and then soaking for an hour in a candlelit bath every night, you probably don't need any advice on de-stressing.

This book is for the people who struggle to find time for a shower, much less a bath. The ones who are still clicking their mouse or ironing a shirt at 11:30 p.m. The ones (and there are thousands of them) who don't take their full yearly vacation and worry that stress is affecting their health and relationships. Or they would if they weren't so tired and that report wasn't due in at 9 a.m.

There is a way of turning brushing your teeth into a meditation and you'll find it here.

But you won't find anything about adopting the lotus position, or yoga, and not too much about giving up coffee and living on mung beans for the rest of your life. Not, of course, because these strategies don't work: They work exceptionally well. But they are not easy and work best if you have a ton of time to "work on yourself." They breed the idea of perfectionism—if you don't do your half hour of yoga each morning, the day's a waste. And we don't need any more of that nonsense. What we need are simple ways of dealing with stress that don't take much more effort than reading this book. And that's what you've got.

When you understand the impact stress has on your body, it's easy to take measures that disperse that stress pronto. You become better at nipping the stressors in the bud—just as you nip the chances of getting dysentery in the bud by choosing not to drink dirty, smelly water.

You'll find ways of dealing with extreme stress here—the sort of stress that axes your life. If stress has been creeping up on you gradually there are ways of defusing months' worth of stress in a few hours. But at the end of the day, stress is an active, not a passive, pursuit. Studies have shown that most of us, just like Rosalind, know how to relax but can't be bothered to do it. So don't just read, but act. Most of these ideas sound embarrassingly simple but they work on a profound level—if you do them. The only way that you can possibly become a more relaxed and less stressed person is to do more that relaxes you and less that stresses you. Self-evident you might think, but not to all of us.

Stress will find you. You can't avoid it. Stress is a fact of life. We can make some of it go away, we can ignore some of it, but eventually we will have to deal with it. Here are some ways of dealing with it fast. And without the lotus position.

1

Let's get positive

So you're stressed? Be grateful. Stress makes life a lot sweeter when you learn to manage it right.

Better sex, sharper mind, longer life—stress does all this. Which is why so many of us are addicted to it.

Nearly half of people report being more stressed today than they were five years ago; over three-quarters of people consider stress intrinsic to their jobs. But let's look at the positives. Some stress is good. Some stress is necessary.

Let's get to the nitty-gritty: Chronic stress over a period of months is detrimental; feeling a little "stressy" once or twice a week is just the ticket. Here's what that level of stress can do for you:

Stress keeps you young
When you're stressed your adrenal glands produce a hormone called dehydroepiandrosterone—known as DHEA to its friends—that has been shown to keep mice alive longer. It was also noted that the same mice had more luxuriant coats. The hormone is thought to build collagen and elastin (the building bricks of the skin) and this stimulates a younger-looking appearance. (The beauty industry

Here's an idea for you... **Relaxation is easier in the dark. Any time you need to de-stress instantly, put your palms over your eyes, shut them, and imagine you are enveloped in black velvet.**

has latched onto this and is trying to develop products that contain DHEA. You're ahead of the game if you produce your own.)

Stress makes you smart

DHEA makes your mind sharper. Chronic stress makes you forgetful but short-term stress can make your brain work better for short periods.

Stress lifts your mood

If you're feeling down in the dumps, a bit of stress isn't necessarily terrible. It could be just what you need to perk you up again. Stress forces you to make decisions and take responsibility. Experts believe this protects us from falling into a state of depression. A recent study found that small doses of the stress hormone cortisol protect some people against depression in the same way that antidepressants regulate mood. Too much cortisol leads to extreme exhaustion, but just a little bit is fine.

Stress improves your sex life

Let's hear it for our old friend, DHEA. Women with a low libido who were given doses of DHEA got more interested again. It turns out that low levels of stress are linked to control of sex drive. Moderate stress releases DHEA and this affects libido positively.

Stress keeps you alive

A study carried out at the University of Texas showed that people with few pressures are up to 50 percent more likely to die within ten years of quitting work than those who faced major responsibility. People under regular pressure tend to take better control of their lives and as a result suffer fewer conditions linked to failing finances, poor relationships, and employment problems.

Stress works in another way to keep us healthy and alive. Humans are designed to have short, sharp periods of stress every now and then. Stress gives us the "high" that is necessary for psychological good health. If your life is free of

Turn to IDEA 22, *Are you too stressed to be happy?*, to discover if your stress levels are dangerous.

Try another idea...

stress you may look to get the highs elsewhere and as result indulge in what psychologists call "high-risk behavior." Translation: extreme sports, football hooliganism, drugs. One way of seeing each of these activities is a way of artificially introducing stress into an understimulated life. Stress keeps us from falling into bad, or crazy, habits.

WE LIED

Life is innately stressful—you can't completely stress-proof your life. Even if you lock yourself in your bedroom for the foreseeable future, stress will find you. Stress is caused by change, and life changes even if you withdraw from it and hide under the bed. The ripples of change will still lap against your bedroom door.

But by learning to manage stress, and use it to your advantage, you can find it motivates, energizes, and spurs you on to a richer and more fulfilling life. And read this idea whenever it's getting you down. Remember, there's only one thing worse for you than too much stress, and that's too little.

"I took a speed reading course and read War and Peace *in 20 minutes—it involves Russia."*
WOODY ALLEN

Defining idea...

How did it go?

Q   We are so stressed that there are no positives. Improve our sex life? We can't even remember what sex is. We're always too exhausted. Where do we start?

A   *The problem is that you're not managing your stress. Here's an idea that is recommended by relationship counselors to stressed couples—get stressed together. At the moment, you're feeling out of control. Take back control and strengthen the bond between you at the same time by setting a goal that you can both strive for. Plan to move, take a trip, have a baby. It sounds counterintuitive but working toward a dream—even a stress-inducing dream—will mean you're in it together and that's de-stressing in itself.*

Q   How do you know when you're stressed positively as opposed to stressed dangerously?

A   *It's really easy. Are you having fun? There's nothing wrong with being busy as long as you are loving your life, are never ill, have fabulous relationships with people who love and support you, and are never afflicted with the suspicion that you are getting your life all wrong. If you are wandering serenely through life, laughing merrily as fortune's outrageous slings and arrows bounce off you, absolutely content with all your decisions, then you can stop reading this now. You may be stressed but you're managing it well.*

2

Find an hour a day to play

No, seriously, is that too much to ask?

Shut your eyes. Breathe deeply. Picture what you'd do today if you had a whole hour each day to yourself to spend doing exactly what you wanted.

"Yeah, right," I hear you say. Like there's any chance of that.

HERE'S A QUESTION WORTH ASKING

I think that the "desirable" things we'd like to spend an hour doing fall into two categories:

- The stuff we yearn to do because it's relaxing and fun

- The stuff that's usually prefixed with a sense of "ought to" because we know the rewards are worth it

In the first category is lying in bed watching a movie; in the second is going for a run or quality time with the kids. We need to find the time for both. But both categories tend to get pushed to the sidelines of our life because of general business.

Here's an idea for you...

On the move and stressed? Running cold water over your wrists for a minute cools you down on a hot day and it works to bring down your stress levels, too.

Exercise especially is one of the things that goes by the wayside when life gets stressful. How many times have you said "I'd love to go to the gym—but I don't have the time." So here's the useful question to ask yourself: How will I feel in five years' time if I don't?

More to the point—how will you look?

Nothing in your life will change unless you take action. If you don't take the time to exercise, if you consistently allow family and work demands to be more important than your continuing good health, then at best you'll be more vulnerable to illness; at worst you'll be fat (and still more vulnerable to illness).

This goes for life dreams that fall into the first category, like writing a novel or learning Russian. These have been called "depth activities" because they add meaning to our lives. If I had a fiver for every time someone said to me "I'd love to write a book but I don't have the time," I wouldn't be writing this one. Wannabe authors miss the point that in just an hour a day, you can make a start. Here's the big question: How will you feel in five years' time if you haven't at least tried?

People who spend at least a little of their time doing the stuff that they want to do tend to feel that they're in control, and that's majorly de-stressing.

FIRST GET THE BIG PICTURE...

Get out your planner and write down everything you're expected to make happen in the next month. This could take some time. Include everything from work projects, organizing babysitters, buying birthday presents, decorating the bathroom, tuning up the car, medical appointments.

OK, finished? Now, go through the list and mark the items that you can delegate to someone else. Be honest. What I said was the items you *can* delegate, not the ones that no one else wants to do, or the ones that no one else will do as well as you. Don't worry. I'm not going to make you hand over all these tasks, just 10 percent of them.

In the spirit of solidarity, I've done this, too. And guess what? On a list of thirteen things only two of them have to be done by me. Actually, only one—writing this book. (I could ask someone else to do it but the publishers might notice; or maybe they wouldn't, which is an even scarier thought.) The other one is to take my youngest for an injection and I could even delegate this if I wanted. But I don't. By actively thinking about it and deciding that it's something I want to do I've turned it into a positive—a choice rather than a chore. Big difference.

Read IDEA 13, *Achieve life–work balance in 10 minutes*, for more on achieving equilibrium.

Try another idea...

"Life is what happens to you when you are busy making other plans."
JOHN LENNON

Defining idea...

Now that you've off-loaded 10 percent of your work for the next month, think about dumping 10 percent of what you have to do every day. Jot down your tasks for tomorrow. Quickly, without thinking too much, run through them marking each entry.

A   Must do
B   Should do
C   Could do

Now knock two of the Bs off the list and three of the Cs off and put down in their place an activity that you know would de-stress you or add depth to your life. Mark it with a big, bold A. Soon, giddy with success, you'll be prioritizing yourself all of the time. Well, at least for an hour a day. Life really is too short to wallow in the C-list—feeling busy but achieving nothing that matters.

Q **I've tried delegating. I've tried prioritizing. I am manic. There is no way I have time to give myself an hour a day. Just how am I going to find the time?**

How did it go?

A *Here's the brutal truth. Only a very small proportion of people are in that boat. For round-the-clock caregivers for the chronically ill, it's hard. For the rest of us, it's not rocket science. Please believe that an hour a day for yourself isn't too much to ask. I don't say that you won't have to give up something to find an hour for yourself. And that might be your sense of being the perfect mother/father/housekeeper/entrepreneur.*

Q **You're kidding—I told you, I'm frantic. Where's the time for this going to come from?**

A *Be creative. I know a high-flying PR director who leaves for work to catch the 7:45 train every morning. Except she doesn't have to catch the 7:45 to make work in time. She catches the 8:15. She spends 30 minutes on the platform reading a novel. That's her only possible break in the day.*

Q **What do I need an hour a day for?**

A *To nourish your soul. I agree that none of this seems particularly worthwhile if you don't have a strong idea of what you want to do with that hour. What makes you feel good? What intrigues you? What makes you say "Oh, I'd love to do that if I only had the time"?*

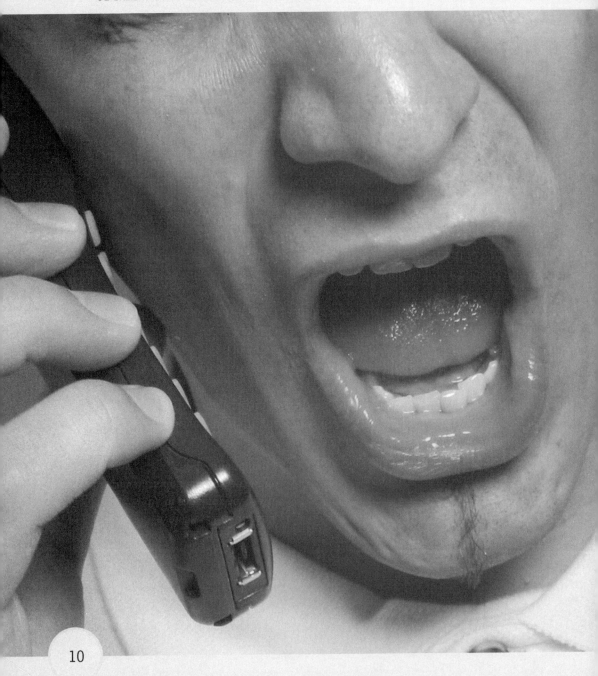

3

Cure yourself of the "disease to please"

Make "just say no" your new mantra.

A huge amount of stress is caused by the inability to say no. Result? We end up driven by other people's agendas.

This is traditionally seen as a female problem. But I'm not so sure. On Saturday night I had dinner with a male friend who told me that for the first time in his ten-year marriage, he'd managed to get his wife to agree to going on vacation on their own without inviting at least two other families. Extreme? Yes. But I know many men whose entire domestic life is run by their partner's agenda and who feel that somehow they're being a bad dad or husband if they say no to the relentless socializing, child-centered activities, and projects set up for them by their driven other halves. I also know men who don't want to stay at work until 8:30 most nights, or go to the bar for an hour on the way home, but can't say no to the pervading culture of their workplace.

Here's an idea for you...

If you just can't say no, try an intermediate stage. Next time someone asks you to do something, say: "I'm not sure, let me get back to you." The breather is often enough to stiffen your resolve.

Now and then, all of us have to do things that don't benefit us much in order to feel that we're pulling our weight. But if it's a daily occurrence then we're going to get rundown and ill. Worse, we're going to get seriously fed up.

Try this quiz. Answer true or false to each of these questions:

I can't relax until I finish all the things I have to do   T/F

If I wasn't doing favors for other people most days, I wouldn't think much of myself   T/F

I seldom say no to a work colleague or family member who asks a favor of me   T/F

I often find myself changing my own plans or working day to fit in with other people's wants   T/F

I rarely, if ever, feel comfortable with what I've accomplished   T/F

I often feel I'm so exhausted that I don't have time for my own interests   T/F

I feel guilty relaxing   T/F

I find myself saying yes to others when inside a voice is saying no, no, no   T/F

I honestly believe that if I stop doing things for others they'd think less of me   T/F

I find it hard to ask other people to do things for me   T/F

Vernon hills
847 634 3650

Add up the number of Ts you scored. If your score is between 7 and 10, you think it's more important to please others than please yourself. If it's between 4 and 6, you should be careful. You're on the slippery slope to terminal niceness. If your score is 3 or less, you're good at saying no and keep your own needs in balance with others.

For some reason, de-cluttering is great for making you feel assertive. Turn to IDEA 23, *Purge your home in a weekend*, for some inspiration.

Try another idea...

DVD'S 4th

renew
Book 3 due 7th
strengthsfinder
Catching fire
searchinside
yourself 7th
9th
5

Aim for a score less than 3. Here are some ways to get there:

1. List your top ten no's, the things you want to eliminate from your life. Start each sentence with "I will no longer..."

2. Think of situations where you need to say no to improve your life. Imagine yourself in these situations saying no. Practice the exercise in front of a mirror if necessary. (This is great. I tried it myself and the experience of actually saying no out loud, albeit in private, makes it much easier in real-life situations.)

3. Whenever you're asked to do anything, ask yourself: "Do I really want to do this?" rather than "Should I do this?" If the answer is no, then let someone else pick up the baton.

"I cannot give you the formula for success, but I can give you the formula for failure, which is: Try to please everybody."
HERBERT BAYARD SWAPE, journalist

Defining idea...

How did it go?

Q   This is all well and good. But who will do it if I don't?

A   *It just may not get done. In an ideal world I'd love to be a hugely successful journalist; a mother who spends hours of quality time with her children; a beautifully dressed, 100 percent fit style icon; and a perfect partner. Oh, and a wonderful friend. I'd love to be top of the class in my college course. And I'd love a perfectly clean home. But it's just NOT POSSIBLE so I decide what's important. Start by asking the question "What can only I do that absolutely has to be done?" For most of us, that list is small. Really small. Everything else is up for grabs. By someone else.*

Q   My life is complicated. There are so many things that I want to do and be involved in, I don't want to say no. Where do I start?

A   *The most useful thing is to work out what life coaches call your "core values"—the things that are really important to you—then put them in order of importance. And then devote regular focused attention to these people and activities. These are the non-negotiables. Everything else is a potential "maybe." This list can change. For instance, my non-negotiables are time with my children and time with my partner. Other priorities are fluid. This year it's studying but last year it was work, as I was supporting my family. So I said no to my friends, to our local school, to my volunteer work, and on occasions, to my extended family. That one hurt—but I just couldn't make every family party. Now I can. Priorities change.*

4

Never procrastinate again

Procrastination is stress's best friend. It's not helpful, but for most of us, it's a way of life.

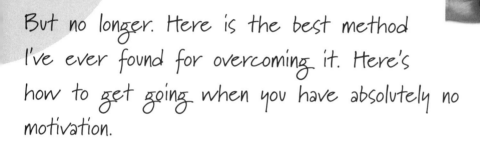

But no longer. Here is the best method I've ever found for overcoming it. Here's how to get going when you have absolutely no motivation.

It was taught to me by life coach Mark Forster. An interesting man, he achieves more in a day than most of us do in a week. But he used to be disorganized and chaotic (he says!). None of the advice on procrastination ever worked for him (we all know that feeling), so he invented his own techniques. (You can read more in his book *Get Everything Done*.)

Mark calls this the rotation method. You need pen, paper, and a watch, but a kitchen timer with a bell works best.

Here's an idea for you...

Scan your planner for big projects coming up. Tomorrow spend just 10 minutes working on each project. By giving a tiny amount of focused attention regularly to projects, well in advance, you accomplish them without even noticing.

1. First, make a list of your tasks. (Here is my list for this morning: Write two ideas for this book, organize dinner party, do washing, make phone calls to pay some bills.)

2. Against each item write 10, 20, 30. These represent blocks of minutes that you are going to spend on each item in turn. So my list would look like:
   Write book 10, 20, 30
   Organize party 10, 20, 30
   Laundry 10, 20, 30
   Phone calls 10, 20, 30

3. Start with the task you most want to do. Set the kitchen timer for 10 minutes. Do the task for 10 minutes. (I choose the laundry—a mindless chore that I enjoy. I have my load in comfortably within the 10 minutes.)

4. When the timer rings, *stop*. Wherever you are in the task. *Stop*. Take a pencil and cross off the 10 next to the task.

5. Set the timer for 10 minutes. Start the next task. (In my case, it's paying bills. It takes me the whole 10 minutes to get the paraphernalia together. Note: I'm no longer resentful about paying the bills, I'm irritated that I can't finish it.)

6. Score through the 10 on the list and start the next task. (Writing. The task that is most formidable, but buoyed by the fact that I've started on the mundane tasks, I sit down, make some notes, and start typing. The timer rings mid-sentence. Note: I'm disappointed that I have to leave my task and move on.)

7. Cross off 10 and start the next task. (I look through recipe books for 10 minutes and make some notes on who to invite.)

Procrastinators often tend to be perfectionists–they can't start because they have to get it right. IDEA 14, *The perfection trap*, has more on this.

Try another idea...

8. Cross off 10 minutes. Now move on to the first task again but set the timer for 20 minutes. Repeat the entire process.

(Laundry again. The first load isn't finished, so I sort the laundry so that it's ready to go in the machine. That takes 10 minutes but I cross off the 20 next to laundry since there's nothing more I can do. I set the egg timer to 20 minutes for the bills. For most of that time I listen to Handel's *Water Music* played on a xylophone but I am halfway through paying the last bill when the timer goes off. Cross off 20. I move back to the writing with a sense of relief—that's the job that's most important but because of my 10-minute start I'm raring to go. When the timer goes off after 20 minutes, I go back to the party, finalize the guest list, and decide on the menu. Back to the laundry—30 minutes. Unload and hang out the washing, start the next load—well within the 30 minutes that they have now been allocated. Now I go back to my computer and complete another 30 minutes. After 30 minutes I pause and look at my list. All the chores have been completed. I don't need to do any more on the party—I've made a real start. And I'm where I want to be—sitting at my computer and enjoying writing, so I set my timer for 40 minutes and continue, promising myself a cup of tea at the end. I'm so into it after 40 minutes that I bring the cup of tea back to my desk and keep going until lunchtime.

"Procrastination is the art of keeping up with yesterday."
DON MARQUIS, humorist

Defining idea...

WHY THIS WORKS FOR ME WHEN NOTHING ELSE DOES

■ It helps you overcome resistance. You can assign a task 5 minutes to begin with—although I started on 10 here. Anybody can do just about anything for 5 minutes.

■ It has a built-in end effect. This is the phenomenon well observed in employees in the two days before going on vacation—they get more done in two days than they usually achieve in a month. The rotation method keeps you focused because you build in artificial deadlines. In other words, you'll get more done in three 20-minute blocks than in an hour of unfocused grind.

■ It has an innate momentum of its own. The easy tasks propel you into the difficult ones.

Q   **Isn't this rotation system overly complicated?**

How did it go?

A   *I make it work for me not by making lists but by drawing little balloons, each with a task in it, joined up by arrows that show me which task to go on to next. I write the minute blocks in each balloon. I've even been known to use colored pencils. It's so liberating to lose to-do lists that I get a bit giddy.*

Q   **But why are you giving the same amount of time to writing as to your laundry?**

A   *By not having endless amounts of time to spend on the important tasks, you get itchy to get on with them. Of course, it was more important for me to write the book than do the laundry but by forcing myself to do the writing I was very focused when I was at my desk. (If you're a chronic procrastinator, just think how that would feel? Fabulous, is the answer.) But just suppose the task you were procrastinating over was your tax return. If you gave it 45 minutes to begin with, you'd never do it. But what if you gave it 5 minutes and watching TV the same weight. Do you see how you could just about bear to get started?*

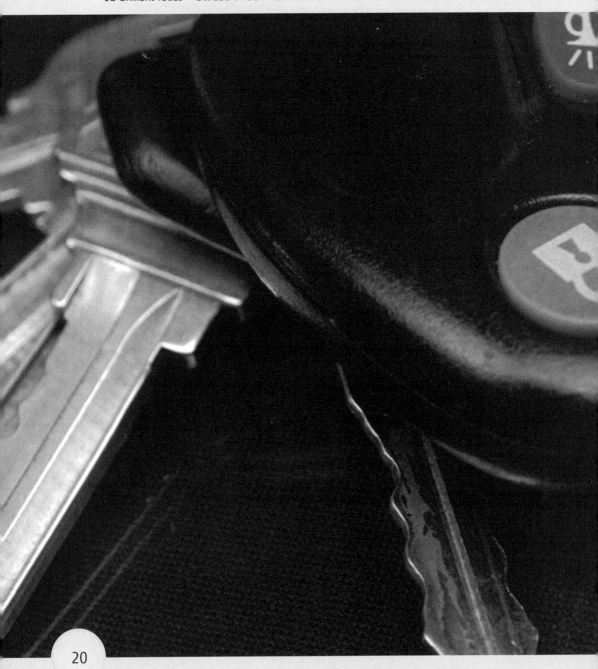

5

Never lose your keys again

Often you can't remember where you left the car keys.
Sometimes you can't remember where you left the car.

Here's why stress eats your memory—and what you can do about it.

Memory lapses aren't necessarily the first indication of Alzheimer's, so don't worry. But if they're increasing in frequency it could be that your memory is a casualty of a multitasking lifestyle.

Juggling a hectic schedule can have a disastrous effect on your memory. The fight-or-flight response actually sharpens our cognitive abilities. But chronic stress over long periods of time is a different matter. If your mind is bustling ahead to deal with the day's problems it's concentrating on other things and you're not noticing what's going on around you. Not surprisingly, you can't retrieve memories of what you did today because your mind was actually living in tomorrow. This in itself is deeply stressful.

WHAT'S HIS NAME AGAIN?

The only answer is to be aware that when you're busy and stressed you're not taking in information in the same way and you're not going to be able to recall it. Make like a Boy Scout and be prepared. For example, on a busy day when you meet

Here's an idea for you...

Try a supplement. There's some evidence that the herb gingko biloba improves blood flow to the brain and hence memory in the elderly, but it's likely that it will be proven to help younger people, too. You can buy supplements containing gingko at drugstores and health food shops. Sage is also good for memory.

someone new, be aware that you are more likely to forget their name. Make more of an effort than usual during introductions. Repeat a new name inside your head. Use it again in conversation as soon as you can.

This repetition is important. When learning anything new during a stressed period, repeat it to yourself and if possible say it out loud three or four times, increasing the amount of time between each repetition. This "repetition, pause, repetition" pattern strengthens memory.

This technique also works for items or tasks that you have to remember and always forget. If you're fed up with going to the supermarket to buy tomatoes and coming back with everything else but tomatoes, try the above. If it doesn't work, then make allowances and leave notes in your purse or on your toothbrush, places where you will certainly check. Don't rely on your memory.

WHERE ARE MY KEYS?

What few people realize is that most routine actions will cause memory problems if you do them differently every day. The very fact that we do some things over and over again can make them easy to forget. That's because when you put items you use frequently in different places from one day to the next, you have to block the memory of what you did with them yesterday and the day before in order to find them today. Which is why it seems like you've spent half of your lifetime looking for your keys and wallet.

The answer

The easiest thing is to create a memory pot—a bowl or basket near your front door where everything goes as soon as you get home, and which you check before you leave the house. This is not as simple as it sounds—it takes about two or three weeks before it becomes second nature. And even then, it makes sense to keep a spare set of keys somewhere separately.

IDEA 25, *Hug your home*, will help you create the order that makes these systems easier.

Try another idea...

DID I TURN OFF THE IRON?

The phenomenon of worrying endlessly if you've done something that you've done a hundred times before is something called "social misattribution," the fancy name for recalling the action but not realizing that you performed it on another occasion. Again, it's because you're not focusing on the action while you're doing it.

The answer

No matter how tied up your brain is with problems, take the time to check what you're wearing. As your arm reaches out to turn off the iron, note "Oh yes, blue shirt." When you get the doubt that you've done an action, recall what your arm was wearing when you did it. Look down. Blue shirt. Check. On you go with your day. Again, just like the above habit, it takes about two or three weeks for this to become second nature when we're undertaking all those activities that we do on automatic pilot—locking the front door, switching off the oven, picking up the children…OK, scratch the last one.

"Happiness is nothing more than good health and a bad memory."
ALBERT SCHWEITZER

Defining idea...

How did it go?

Q **When I'm stressed I forget what I want to say next. How can I avoid embarrassing myself during presentations?**

A *As someone who hates public speaking of any sort, I sympathize. There is a phenomenon called "state dependent retrieval," which means when you're stressed out, you get into a physiological state that is different from the relatively calm one you were in when you acquired the information. In other words if you're nervous enough, you'll forget your mother's name. Notes and visual gimmicks that immediately take you back to what you are saying are essential. I'd also recommend that you spend time going over and over what you want to say, ideally in front of an audience (by that I mean your partner or friend). This will help immeasurably but because of state dependent retrieval, success isn't always guaranteed. However, being well prepared does make you less nervous. And eventually giving seamless presentations builds your sense of self-esteem to such a point that you stop panicking.*

Q **As I get older I do forget where I've left the car. It's no joke. Should I be worried?**

A *No. But if you find yourself forgetting what your car is for, then it's time to have a chat with your doctor (assuming you can remember who she is)!*

6

What's your plan B?

Take the insecurity out of your life. All you need is a plan B.

It could be your best friend in stressed-out times.

The life you're living is plan A. Plan B is what happens if it all goes to hell in a handbasket. Know how you'd get from A to B and you remove a huge chunk of the stress that is caused by worry about the future.

It was a former boss who taught me the value of having a plan B. Magazine editors have one of the most glamorous jobs going—great pay, company car, free vacations, free clothes...

And they have one of the most insecure jobs you can imagine. The higher they climb, the faster they can fall. Their job is highly stressful and they routinely work their butts off for an employer only to be shunted to the side in a matter of hours if they don't deliver. "How do you stand it?" I asked my former boss. "Always, always have a plan B," she told me breezily.

Here's an idea for you...

Tomorrow open a completely new bank account for your plan B. Start a direct debit and pay in until you've built up your emergency fund total to three months' expenses. Knowing you've got enough money to finance your dream makes your present life a whole lot more fulfilling.

DECIDING ON PLAN B

Every life has its fair shares of upsets and reversals of fortune. An essential of the plan B is to be able to look at your life dispassionately and see potential stress lines—where your life is likely to come apart. For instance:

- If you work in a volatile industry, it's work. Your plan B is what you'll do if your dismissal slip lands on your desk.

- If your relationship is struggling, your plan B is what you'll do if you split up.

- If your health isn't good, your plan B is to research methods of financing your life if bad stuff happens.

Now please, don't get upset. I'm not trying to rain on your parade or say that your happy world is about to fall down around you. I'm merely concerned with stress-proofing your life, and plan Bs are great for this. No one says you'll ever need plan B but having one is an invaluable comfort when you wake in the middle of the night and can't get back to sleep because of catastrophic thoughts swirling around in your brain. You know those nights? Well, with a plan B, you worry for about 30 seconds, go "Oh, I remember, I've got a plan B," roll over, and doze off again.

For plan B to work it has to be a fantasy built on reality. By that I mean it's not just a vague "Oh, I'll sell the house and move to France." It's more concrete than that.

BUILDING THE DREAM

First, decide on your plan B and start a file. Add clippings, pictures, information to it. Suppose you were going to sell your house and move to France. Your file for this would include information on people who had done the same thing, and research on how much you'd need to live on per year in France if you were mortgage-free. You'd also put in notes on the school system if you have young children.

Your plan B should be realistic, but it should be awesome. It shouldn't be a case of "Oh well, I could always move back in with Mom." It should be training to become a chef, starting your own business, backpacking around Mexico. It should make your heart sing. Plan realistically but dream big.

BUILDING AN EMERGENCY FUND

Think about the financial position you'd need to be in to make it work, and take steps to achieve it. The ideal sum for a "just-in-case fund," whatever your plan B, is eight months' worth of living expenses. Go through your bank statements, adding up your expenses for a year—this is truly frightening—take the total, divide by twelve to get your average per month, and then multiply by eight.

Still reeling? Yes, it does that have effect. OK, eight months is ideal but it's that—an ideal.

De-cluttering is great for helping you focus. Try IDEA 30, *Zap those piles*, for some hints on this.

Try another idea...

"Reality is the leading cause of stress amongst those in touch with it."
JANE WAGNER and LILY TOMLIN, comic writers

Defining idea...

27

However, I'd say that a priority for anyone who wants to stress-proof their life is to build up at least three months' living expenses. That's the bare minimum that you should have easily accessible in a bank account according to the experts.

What happens when you spend more of your time thinking about plan B than worrying about plan A? Then it's time to move your life on.

How did it go?

Q   **So you're saying that you should start any enterprise imagining failure. Is it necessary to be so pessimistic?**

A   *Dream big dreams by all means. Be single-minded. Fight for plan A. But don't stick too rigidly to just one idea of how you can be happy. Flexibility makes it more certain that you'll be one of life's winners and that you'll deal with stress successfully along the way.*

Q   **When do you give up on your plan A? I am struggling on with my plan A (writing a novel). It's going well but it's taking much longer than I thought. Should I grow up and get a job (plan B)?**

A   *Good question. Your plan A may be terrific but if it's too stressful, it will eventually tell on your body. If you're becoming depressed or experiencing any of the other physical symptoms of stress then perhaps it's time to start taking on part of plan B. But remember if your plan B is to go back to paid work, it doesn't need to be a full-on five-day-a-week career. What about working locally three times a week to boost your income but allow you plenty of writing time? Plan B's are your choice and they should be inspiring you as much as plan A's. They don't work otherwise.*

7

Off the payroll

Only one thing gets you down, and hence stressed, more than work. Not working.

For periods when you're "resting," or times when you're not earning, you need this idea.

Paradoxically, one of the most stressed periods of any life is when you don't have to worry about the 9 to 5 because for whatever reason you're no longer in paid employment.

People in low-paid, menial jobs are far more stressed than thrusting type-A folks. They have little control over their working life and there's nothing more stressful than lack of control. Those laid off or who are between jobs, women who have had children and opted to stay at home—anyone, basically, who doesn't get paid (note, I didn't say who doesn't work) is vulnerable to the stress of the "no work" phenomenon.

What's the answer?

Here's an idea for you...

Aim for excellence. You may be an adequate cook. Use your time off to become a fantastic one. You may love reading. Become an exemplary reader. List all those classic novels you've been meaning to read but never got around to.

TAKE CONTROL

If you're looking for a job, don't fritter away time worrying while making halfhearted or piecemeal attempts to find one. You need a strategy. You need short-term and long-term goals. You need to break these goals down into tasks and you need to schedule these tasks in your planner. You know this. It's just that when you're anxious it's a lot easier to spend hours fine-tuning your résumé and waiting for the phone to ring than to be proactive.

Call every contact you know. Look into part-time or casual work that will at least give you some money until you get a job. At the end of the day having lists of tasks completed will give you a sense of achievement and help you feel in control. Enlist a friend if necessary. The hardest thing in the world is to call ten contacts and sell yourself to them, but asking a friend to call you at the end of the day to check that you've done it is a powerful motivator.

If you're a mother at home with children, structure is vital. Set yourself personal goals—just like you did at work. These goals should not just be about the children. Getting a boost from "achieving" with the kids instead of "achieving" in the workplace is fine when they're really small, but your sense of displacement and low self-esteem may be greater when they grow up a bit, even if you have no regrets about the time you've lavished on them.

BUILD CONFIDENCE

Here's a difficult tip but one that really works. Ask five people that know you well to answer these questions honestly;

A calm environment helps if you're at home a lot. Try IDEA 23, *Purge your home in a weekend.*

Try another idea...

- What is the first thing you think of when you think of me (immediately cut out anyone who says "unemployed")?

- What do you think is the most interesting thing about me?

- What do you think has been my greatest accomplishment?

- What do you value most about me?

- What do you perceive to be my greatest strengths?

OK. A little embarrassing. But just say you've been asked to answer these questions on a job application and you're (becomingly, modestly) stuck for ideas. What you'll be amazed at is the different perceptions people have of you. It also helps you realize that qualities you take for granted aren't qualities that everyone shares. You're unique.

"You take my life when you do take the means whereby I live."
WILLIAM SHAKESPEARE,
The Merchant of Venice

Defining idea...

GET HAPPY

When you're short on money, isolated, and bored, it's unlikely that you're getting the regular doses of endorphins that we need to stay happy campers. Understimulation leads to fatigue and depression. It's essential to manufacture highs and you have to do it daily. Make a "joy list" of things that will give you a sense of achievement and happiness that don't cost a lot. By slotting them regularly into your day, you'll fire off endorphins and fool your body that you are still a highflier with endless cash to fritter away on life's inanities. You could decide to start every day with an alfresco breakfast, spend an afternoon watching a movie, or have a glass of wine under the stars. Every day must have one pure pleasure.

Q **I've been spending my between-jobs period looking for a new job in the morning and writing a film script in the afternoon. I'm being productive. Why am I so depressed?**

How did it go?

A *It's very hard to keep the faith when you get no palpable payback. In my opinion—and it's only my opinion—it's worth including a few activities that have definite payoffs recognized as worthwhile by society. Doing charity work usually means others recognize you as a pretty good person. Working weekends as a cabdriver earns you cash. Less useful for this is writing your novel or launching your career as a portrait painter or looking after your children, because society isn't good at recognizing that these are worthwhile yet (although the last is changing slowly). These activities are not a waste of time but the fruit of your labor is purely subjective and in time doing them exclusively makes you feel isolated and defensive. Do the things you've always wanted to do by all means but also do some that will definitely result in rewards recognized by everyone.*

Q **I've been looking for a job for a year, but haven't been offered enough money to make it worth my while to switch off the TV. Why do I have no interest?**

A *You sound depressed. If your house is either a mess or anally tidy, I'm prepared to bet on it. Actually, the "get happy" advice can work well for anyone with moderate depression if you give it a try but if you've only got enough willpower to flick the remote it might be just too much. All I can ask you is "What's the alternative?" Without looking for help, nothing will change. Speak to your doctor or seek out counseling.*

8

A zone of your own

Imagine a place with no phone, no noise, no hassle, no problems.

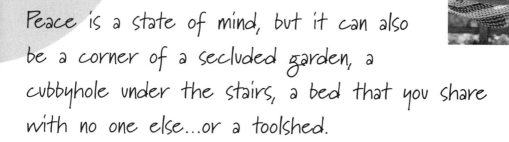

Peace is a state of mind, but it can also be a corner of a secluded garden, a cubbyhole under the stairs, a bed that you share with no one else...or a toolshed.

My "own" space is the garden shed and that's where I'm writing this. I live in a tiny, inner-city apartment with three other people and it's impossible, short of locking myself in the bathroom, for me to be alone—and even then it won't be for long.

Mine is not one of those structures found in magazine articles where they interview people who work in "sheds" at the end of their yard, and the shed turns out to be a fully equipped study, costing several arms and legs. Mine is quite literally a common or garden shed variety, so small that it wasn't even much good for storage, and so ugly that we nearly got rid of it when we moved in.

But since we gave it a makeover it looks great. It is painted a soft white inside, with a wall shelved and devoted to my favorite research books, and room for a tiny desk,

Here's an idea for you...

Write down what taste, scent, sensation, sound, and sight immediately relaxes you and gather them in one place so they are always at hand. Velvet slippers, satin quilts, birdsong, pink light, roses. What sensual cues calm you down instantly?

a comfortable chair, a sheepskin rug, a radio, and a vase of flowers. When I'm inside it, it has all I need. I use it to get some peace to write, or just to sit and read quietly. In the summer I sit in the doorway with a cup of tea and listen to the birdsong. In the winter, I bring a blanket, light candles, and cozy down to read a chapter of a book.

Having a place you can call your own helps immeasurably with stress. I realized this after reading a book about sacred and meditation rooms around the world. The need for a quiet place is universal. I was intrigued by the ingenuity of those who clearly lived in the real world like me, where knocking out the center of the house to build an atrium wasn't really an option. One woman had turned a fair-sized closet into her own sanctuary and filled it with objects significant to her. I was particularly taken by a sweet Sikh who kept his shrine on a breakfast tray and simply stuck it in a closet when it wasn't being used. (It was beautiful, too.)

Why bother? Because I think that in some very profound way having a corner where you can let your imagination run free and where you have control is deeply important to the human spirit. As a child did you have a secret place where you would hide away? Did you build "shrines"? No? Think of the times you set up your favorite toys next to your bed, your dolls aligned looking just right on a shelf, "special" power stones hidden in a secret place only you knew about? Children love talismans and can spend hours contemplating a feather, a flower, a broken bottle. This is how they de-stress away from their parents, in a world of their own where they choose objects that soothe them and where they decide their significance— not the grown-ups.

Creating a place where you can go that is uniquely yours, where you have chosen what you look at, what you feel, hear, and smell will prove invaluable in your battle against stress. A room is ideal, a closet will do, a corner of a room—just one armchair will be enough. There you are in control and you can read, rest, dream, just be. It could be a seat in your garden, a daybed in the spare room, a dressing table, or simply a shelf or windowsill on which a simple cerulean vase holding a pink rose sits. But it should be so attractive to you that you long to sink into your sanctuary—that way you'll want to carve out a little time for yourself as often as possible so you can be there. And that's the essence of relaxation.

Read about the bath ritual in IDEA 28, *Turning Japanese*, to discover how to create a sanctuary in your bathroom.

Try another idea...

"You need a break from the frantic, noisy, overpopulated world. And permission to write, read, rest, draw, do yoga, listen to music, sit, and stare—anything that evokes the deepest, most peaceful part of you."
O MAGAZINE

Defining idea...

How did it go?

Q   **You've got a shed. You're lucky. But I don't even have a backyard, so what are my options?**

A   *You need a portable sanctuary. In some ways this is even better. Prior to the shed, I had a box. Inspired by the "shrine on a tray," I got a nice wooden box and kept a candle scented with gardenia, a beautifully embroidered cushion, a CD of the Brandenburg concertos, and a sheepskin rug to lie on. Just opening this box relaxed me. When all your tools are gathered together it makes it far more likely that you will actually relax because you will hear them "calling you" on busy days.*

Q   **This is all a little too hippie for me. Any other ideas, preferably a bit more down to earth?**

A   *I understand that this talk of shrines could be putting you off. However, I have rarely been in a home that didn't have a shrine somewhere. Family photographs arranged on a mantlepiece form a shrine. The china animals you inherited from your grandmother and lovingly arranged in the dining room are a sort of shrine. All I'm saying is be conscious of these objects because a few minutes caring for and contemplating them each day will realign you with what's important in your life. Dust your photos and perhaps put some fresh flowers next to them every couple of days. Concentrate on what's important to you for a few minutes. That's called "mindful meditation," and it's very good for your stress levels.*

9

Relaxation—what we can learn from the cavemen

There's nothing wrong with stress. We're designed to get stressed. It's how we deal with it that's the problem.

Coping with stress should be simple. My central message to you can be summarized in one sentence. Get stressed—relax.

So why are we facing an epidemic of stress? The answer lies in the way we interpret the word "relax." Remember that stress developed in order for us to deal with danger. When faced with something that scares us (more likely nowadays to be a to-do list running into double figures rather than the saber-toothed tigers that ate our ancestors), we release adrenaline. This in turn causes the release of noradrenaline and cortisol and these three hormones together sharpen our wits, release energy to our muscles, and divert resources from one part of the body to the parts where you need it most. Which is why you feel twitchy when you're very stressed and can't sit still. The adrenaline coursing through your body would have been just dandy in helping you cope with the saber-toothed tiger but is a bit of an overreaction when your boss has caught you booking your vacation on the Internet rather than working on the sales report.

Here's an idea for you...

Next time you're waiting in a line, or for traffic lights to change, or for the elevator to come, see it as an opportunity for a mini-break. Take some deep breaths, feel the tension flow out of your body and your shoulders drop. People who make an effort to do this report being less stressed in a week.

Anyway. All those hormones get the job done. But then we come to the little-mentioned other side of the stress equation—"relaxation." After fighting off a tiger, or running away from it, our cavemen ancestors would have made their way back to the cave for a rest. There wasn't much to do in the caves. Sit quietly, stare at the walls. Maybe draw on them. Rest and recreation, calm and peace, lots of sleep— sometimes for days. Rest is essential to repair and recover from the effect of stress hormones on our organs. That's what we learned to expect over the course of millennia.

But what do we do now after a stressful day? We are likeliest to celebrate with alcohol, a cigarette, coffee (all of which trigger another stress response). Or even worse, after a stressful situation, we throw ourselves straight into another one. This means that our bodies are bathed in stress hormones for far longer than was ever intended.

The body's hormones work in delicate balance. When the three main stress hormones are fired they affect the levels of all the others, notably insulin (that regulates sugar levels and energy) and serotonin (the happy hormone that affects mood and sleep). When they go awry over long periods of time, the results can be disastrous for our health, both mental and physical.

Which is why we start off stressed and end up stressed, fat, unhappy, and unhealthy.

Try IDEA 14, *The perfection trap*, if you never have time to relax.

Try another idea...

The solution is to build relaxation in to your life, hour by hour, day by day.

Five minutes every hour

See your day not as a long purgatory of stress but as lots of small stress responses punctuated with mini-relaxation breaks. As a rough rule, every waking hour should have five minutes of pleasure. So after every hour of working, take a minimum to do something pleasurable—answer an email, stretch your shoulders, have a cup of tea. Can't leave your desk? Spend a few minutes a day dreaming of something that makes you happy.

Fifteen minutes every day

Practice active relaxation—listening to music, yoga, sex, dancing. TV is passive and doesn't count.

Three hours every week

At least three hours every week should be spent doing an activity you love. It should be calming, and non-work orientated. I make it a rule that it only counts as my three hours if I can do it without makeup. In other words, it doesn't count if it involves people that I feel I have to make an effort with. You will have your own way of judging if it is truly relaxing. Be honest. This cannot be an activity that furthers your career, your ambitions, your children's friendships, or your perfectionist streak.

"In times of stress be bold and valiant."
HORACE

Defining idea...

How did it go?

Q   My way of relaxing is with a glass of wine and the TV. Do I have to give up my glass of cabernet?

A   *Alcohol stresses the body but we're not advocating teetotalism. Oh no. But switching off the TV will help de-stress you. It's a passive form of relaxation, and you need to do something active that depends on your thought processes to relax you: the radio, audiobooks, or simply reading a book are all much better.*

Q   The bar is more relaxing to me than anything else. Being with friends is how I relax. Should I continue this?

A   *OK, all I'm saying is that sitting around in smoky atmospheres and boozing isn't going to switch off your stress hormones any more than slumping in front of the TV. Luckily our prime time for both these activities is our teens and twenties when our bodies are optimally fit and can withstand the hideous toll of being bathed in stress hormones practically 24/7. But if you're in your thirties, or older, you're storing up health problems for the future. Start with the "5 minutes every hour" principle during your working day. Then make a plan for an evening at home where you actively relax. Fill it with all the activities you like to do that don't include switching on a screen. It's a good idea to have one, but preferably two or three evenings like this a week, and staying at home makes it easier to go alcohol-free at least two days a week, which is the expert recommendation. Then think of ways that you can spend time with your friends that doesn't involve bars.*

10

Leave the office on time

Reduce interruptions. Reclaim your evenings.

Take control. Don't let your working day be hijacked by others. The secret is to have your goals clear in your mind.

THINK WEEKLY, THEN DAILY

Don't be a slave to a daily to-do list. See the big picture. On Monday morning lose the sinking "I've got so much to do" sensation. Instead, think "What are my goals for this week?" Decide what you want to have done by Friday and then break each goal into smaller tasks that have to be undertaken to achieve all you want by Friday. Slot these tasks in throughout your week. This helps you prioritize so that the tricky and difficult things, or tasks that depend on other people's input, don't sink to the back of your consciousness. It also means you are giving attention to all that you have to do and not spending too much time on one task at the beginning of the week.

Concentrate on three or four items on your to-do list at once. You won't be overwhelmed.

Here's an idea for you...

Create a "virtual you" if you're getting stressed out in the office by the demands of others. When you're an administrative linchpin, set up a shared file where people can go to find the information or resources they'd usually get from you.

WORK WITH YOUR ENERGY CYCLES

Some of us operate better in the morning, some in the late afternoon. If your job demands creativity, block out your most creative periods so that you can concentrate on your projects. Don't allow them to be impinged upon by meetings and phone calls that could be done anytime.

Make the phone call you're dreading. Right now. That call that saps your energy all day. Just do it.

Have meetings in the morning. People are frisky. They want to whizz through stuff and get on with their day. Morning meetings go much faster than those scheduled in the afternoon.

Check emails three times a day. First thing in the morning, just after lunch, and just before you leave are ideal times. Keeping to this discipline means that you don't use email as a distraction.

Limit phone calls. Talk to other people when it suits you, not them. In my working life I receive around twenty phone calls a day. Answering machines don't help me personally—the call-back list is another chore. This is how I turned it around. The most time-effective way of using the phone is to limit your calls as you do your emails—to three times a day. Make a list of calls you have to make that day. Call first thing. If someone isn't there, leave a message and unless you have to talk to them urgently, ask them to call you back at your next "phone period." Just before lunch is good. That means neither of you will linger over the call. Your other "phone time" should be around 4:30 p.m. for the same reason. Of course, you can't limit phone calls completely to these times but most of us have some control over incoming calls. I don't have a secretary anymore to screen calls, but I very politely say "Sorry, I'm in the middle of something." I tell the caller when I'll be free and most people offer to call me back then, saving me the hassle of calling them. No one minds that if their call isn't urgent. The point of all of this is to keep phone calls shorter by putting them in the context of a busy working day. Social chat is important and nice but most of us spend too much time on it. Time restrictions stop us from rambling on. And this goes for personal calls, too. Check your watch as soon as a friend calls. Give yourself five minutes maximum. Or better still save personal calls as a treat for a hardworking morning.

Combine this with IDEA 38, *Take a vacation at your desk,* **to enjoy the time you do spend in the office more.**

Try another idea...

"Take a note of the balls you're juggling. As you keep your work, health, family, friends, and spirit in the air, remember that work is a rubber ball and will bounce back if you drop it. All the rest are made of glass; drop one of them and it will be irrevocably scuffed, tarnished, or even smashed."
JON BRIGGS, voice-over expert

Defining idea...

45

How did it go?

Q **At the end of the day, I've worked really hard but have only done two things on my list. How can I avoid this soul-destroying feeling?**

A *Chances are you're an underestimator. Most of us are in this category. We seriously underestimate how long each job will take us, we fail to complete it—and so set ourselves up to feel ineffectual. Keeping a time log for a week—even better, for a month—gives you information on how long tasks really take you. Keep a detailed account of what you actually do half hour by half hour during the day for a week. This will give you facts. Deliver more than you promise and people will love you.*

Q **The culture in my office is that we stay late. Even if I got through my work, I'd have to stay. What's the answer?**

A *Different problem. At the end of the day (literally, in this case), it's up to you. If you don't have family commitments, if you have a decent life-work balance, if your health is good, if you think the best use of your time is developing your career, and, MOST IMPORTANT, if you think your hard work will be rewarded, then stay and work. But if not, then it might be time to rethink your priorities or find a new job.*

11

Speed parenting (better than stressed parenting)

Children pick up adult stress like a dry sponge soaks up water.

When you're happy, they're happy. And when you're stressed? Yep, you got it. That's when you need focused parental skills.

Calm parents usually mean calm kids, but when you're frazzled, they reflect it and have a horrible tendency to get bad tempered, argumentative, clingy, and sick.

That's because stress is contagious. You get stressed, your kids get fussy—at best. At worst, they get ill. Most parents know the rule of "reverse serendipity" that guarantees it's on the days when your car gets broken into and your job depends on you delivering a fabulous (and as yet unprepared) presentation that your youngest will throw a fit and hide under his bed refusing to go to school because he's dying.

It's not mere coincidence. Research shows that even when they're tiny, children pick up on their stressed parents' frowns, tense jaws, averted eyes, and other physical signs of stress. In turn, they cry or become withdrawn.

Here's an
idea for
you...

**Next time you talk to a child
get on their level, eye to eye.
They respond better. Kneel
when they're toddlers. Stand on
a stool when they're teenagers.**

Up to the age of about ten, children think their parents' stress is their fault. After that, they're less egocentric and recognize that outside factors cause it, but still, they can feel it's their responsibility to sort out the problem for mom or dad. Parents often applaud this "caretaker role" that children take on because they see it as a sign that their children are growing up to be responsible and caring. But since your twelve-year-old can't possibly stop your boss from firing you or your mother's less-than-endearing habit of reeling around town drunk at 3 p.m., his efforts to lighten your load, although laudable, will only be a partial success. Children discover that their efforts aren't making you happy and that can transfer into adult feelings of guilt and low self-esteem.

SHORT-TERM ANSWER

Explain that you're stressed out, tell them why, but also show them that you're working out a way to handle it. Your competence in the face of a stressful day is an invaluable lesson for later life. Saying "I'm stressed, here's what I'm doing about it," and giving them a timescale of when they can expect you to be back to normal goes a long way to reassuring them.

And on those days when it's all going horribly wrong, your kids are being unbearable and not letting you do what you have to do, then the best advice is to give them what they want—your time. This piece of advice was taught to me by a grandmother and I've been stunned at how well it works. Pleading for an hour of peace won't work, but ten minutes of concentrating on them—a quick game, a talk, a cuddle, and a story—calms them down and they tend to wander off and leave you alone.

Are your kids really pushing your buttons? Check out IDEA 33, *Embrace the dark side.*

Try another idea...

LONG-TERM SOLUTION

Besides demonstrating your competence in handling stress, the other side of stress-proofing your kids is to make them feel secure. The more secure your child is, the better he'll be able to handle stress—even the stress that's caused by you. And the better he'll be at handling stress for the rest of his life.

More than all the myriad advice I've had on child care from child behavioral experts, the most useful was from a taxi driver who told me that since his three children were born he'd always made a point during the working week of spending ten minutes a day with each one of them. Ten minutes a day sounds meager but it's enough—if you actually do it. It's better to be realistic and consistent than to aim for an hour and achieve it only once a week. Even worse is to keep interrupting your time together to take a call from the office. Chat, wash their doll's hair, read a story (Hint: Older children still like being read to)—but treat that ten minutes as sacred.

"There is no way to be a perfect parent, but thousands of ways of being a great one."
ANONYMOUS

Defining idea...

How did it go?

Q **Look, I know what I should do but my life is really stressful. My kids can be very annoying. Often I lose it and scream at them. Am I scarring them for life?**

A *If you lose it very frequently, it's not great—eventually they will start shouting back at you. Which means you'll all be scarred for life. If you don't lose it that often, it's not the end of the world. But even then it's good to say you're sorry. Wait until things calm down and then say "I was wrong to shout at you." If their behavior was fine but stress led to you taking your anger out on them, then your apology should be unequivocal. If there were mitigating circumstances to your anger—they continued baiting you despite warnings to stop, say—still apologize but explain their part in the meltdown.*

Q **My spouse and I haven't been getting along but we've done our best to act normally in front of our children. So why are they so withdrawn?**

A *It's difficult for loving parents to accept that their behavior is in any way harming their children. Beware of pretending too hard that everything is hunky-dory, because even very little kids are very good at acting out their stress in similarly clandestine ways. Other signs that kids are stressed is bullying, sibling fighting, sleeplessness, anxiety, or an inability to perform straightforward tasks such as homework. Speak to a doctor or mental health practicioner. There is a wealth of expert advice available to you but before you can access it, you have to be strong enough to admit there's a problem.*

12

Lost your mojo?

When you're bored, dull, lackluster, you're as stressed as it gets.

What you need is a bit more stress—the positive kind.

Stress gives life piquancy. It gives life verve. Workers who aren't under enough stress are unhappier and unhealthier than those who have stressful, challenging jobs.

For challenge, read control. Because even though it seems a contradiction in terms, stressed people tend to have more control than they realize. And that sense of control is so delicious that most of us go out of our way to bring more stress into our lives, just so we can get the hit.

On the other hand, if your life is lacking in stress—or is quite challenging but you don't get any sense that you are in control—then you will get bored, frustrated, and depressed. You stop thinking you're a good person. You stop thinking you're successful. What they never tell you in all the reams about the evils of stress is that coping with it does wonders for your self-esteem.

Experts believe that our bodies are designed to be mentally and physically stimulated on a daily basis—whether it's running for the bus or meeting tight deadlines. When we put ourselves under stress, we get rewarded for it. When

Here's an idea for you... **Sit back and grin. You'll find a big smile sends the message to your brain to relax even when there's absolutely nothing funny happening.**

forced to perform, our bodies release adrenaline. This triggers feel-good chemicals such as serotonin, which flood our body as a reward for completing a difficult task. Resolving a problem gives us a hormonal buzz and we feel terrific.

If you're bored and fed up with life, you simply might not be stressed enough. It's good to feel that you're competent, striving, achieving. In fact, I'll go further: It's impossible to feel this way without an element of stress unless you're an enlightened Buddhist monk. So if religion isn't your bag, it's imperative to find out what is. You might get your kick from being a Master of the Universe and killing the competition, you might get it from saving a forest of ancient oaks. You might get it from supporting your family without selling your soul. These are the big things, but little ones work, too. There are two important things to do:

1. Recognize what gives you a kick and seek it out
Next time you feel down in the dumps, don't head for the bar or turn to the cookie jar. Get busy and up your stress levels. Set yourself a goal to be achieved by bedtime. Tidying your desk, cooking a perfect soufflé, making two calls you've been dreading. Your body looks to experience the feel-good chemicals regularly. If you're not getting enough adrenaline in your system the danger is that you turn to artificial stimulants such as alcohol, sugary food, or smoking (all of which mimic adrenaline's effect on your body) just to make life more interesting. Unfortunately, booze, sugar, and smoking all age you. Whereas setting yourself challenges keeps you young and vital.

2. Give yourself the space to enjoy the kick

After completing any challenge or stressful act, always, always, always switch off.

Turn to IDEA 22, *Are you too stressed to be happy?*, for more on burnout.

Try another idea...

Remember, you should either be relaxed or stimulated—not both at once. If your body wants to rest after meeting a challenge and you are full of anxiety about what you could or should be doing next, "then your body doesn't know whether it is relaxed and repairing or stimulated and solving," says stress expert Liz Tucker. After achieving a goal, small or large, or after any period of stress—and that includes running for the bus—make sure you take the time to acknowledge the happy hormones. Laugh with a friend, shut your eyes and visualize yourself on a beach, breathe deeply. Mentally congratulate yourself for every achievement, however small. Physically make sure your body knows that you're pleased with yourself.

The reason that people who are regular exercisers are less stressed is because going for a run or whatever each day automatically builds in the reward kick and they feel in control of their lives. If you don't know where to start with this idea, I would strongly recommend you think about exercise. Buy a pedometer and aim to do a few more steps each day until you're averaging 10,000 without much trouble. Or aim for a regular swim and make sure that you reward your body with a sauna or steam afterward. Exercise is great for lending itself to both goal setting and physical rewards.

"This time, like all times, is a very good one, if we but know what to do with it."
RALPH WALDO EMERSON

Defining idea...

How did
it go?

Q   I feel really bored. Not stressed, just overwhelming ennui. What can I do about this?

A   *This is a very simple plan but it might work. Do everything differently today. Brush your teeth with the other hand, walk on the other side of the road to work, if you always smile at your boss, don't. Eat new food that you haven't eaten before. Take a different route home. Physically do it differently and mentally you break out of the rut. This is amazingly powerful. Do something different every day—"change for change's sake"—and you'll tap into creativity and see the world from a new angle. And that should help.*

Q   But I'm deep-down bored with my life. And believe me, I've got plenty of stress. What's the answer?

A   *It sounds like you might have reached burnout phase, where you are so exhausted by stress that it takes something drastic to pull you out of your stressed-out hole. Book a vacation immediately. If after a couple of weeks you still feel depressed, then see your doctor. Don't struggle on alone.*

13

Achieve life-work balance in 10 minutes

I refuse to call it work–life. It should be life–work. And that's what achieving it entails—a lifework.

Unless, of course, you've read this idea.

Just a small point, but have you ever met anyone who felt they've achieved the perfect work–life balance? I've been thinking about it since lunchtime and I'm still struggling to come up with a name.

One of the most pernicious things about stress is the way we don't notice how it switches our attention away from what we value and love in life until it's too late. So here are some clues to figure out if stress is stomping all over your life–work balance...

1. Do you feel like your day is spent dealing with difficult people and difficult tasks?

2. Do you feel that those you love don't have a clue what's going on with you and you don't have a clue what's going on with them?

Here's an idea for you...

Designate Saturday "family" day and Sunday afternoon "selfish" time. We can usually find an hour or so on Sunday afternoon to spend on ourselves–just don't let it get filled with chores or your partner's agenda.

3. Do you regularly make time for activities that nourish your soul?

4. Do you feel you could walk out the door of your house and no one would notice you were gone until the mortgage had to be paid?

Yes, you guessed it, number 3 was the trick question. Answer yes to that one and you're probably all right. Answer yes to the rest and you could be in trouble.

In a nutshell, make sure you're putting time and effort into the people and activities that make your heart sing and it really is very difficult to buckle under the effect of stress.

But I think too much emphasis is put on the stress caused by the "work" part of the equation and not enough placed on the stress caused by the "life" part. Everyone assumes that all we need is less work, more life and all would be in harmonious balance. Hmmm.

Where it has gone all wrong for so many, women especially, is that they've cleared enough time for the "life" part of the equation but not taken into account that it isn't necessarily restful or enjoyable. This is no idle observation. Research shows that men's stress hormones tend to fall when they get home whereas women's stay high after the working day, presumably because they get home to confront a dozen chores and hungry kids. Your children may be the reason you get out of bed in the morning but you need to accept that spending time with them is not necessarily any less stressful than work—in fact, it often makes work seem like a walk in the park. More time with your kids is not necessarily the answer.

IDEA 43, *Perfect moments*, has more about balancing the demands on your life.

Try another idea...

More time with yourself, very probably, is.

That old saying is true—if you don't look after yourself, you can't look after anyone else. And all it takes is just ten minutes a day.

And ten minutes of selfishness every day is enough to make a profound difference in your ability to achieve a life balance that works. Try it.

"The best and safest thing is to keep a balance in your life, acknowledge the great powers around us and in us. If you can do that, and live that way, you are really a wise man."
EURIPIDES

Defining idea...

How did it go?

Q I feel I probably get it right one week a month. How can I get it right all of the time?

A *Have a very clear list in your head of what is important to you. Instead of abstract virtues (integrity, passion), figure out your different roles and their importance in your life. My roles at the moment are: wife, mother, employee, author, student, counselor, daughter, sister, friend... You get the idea, now jot down yours. Stop at ten. Then prioritize them. You won't always stick to this order but it will give you a working template that you can use when you are running around like a headless chicken and don't know where to turn.*

Q How does this work in practice?

A *OK. Today I have a choice. I could stay in the office and work, or get home in time to read stories. "Mother" comes higher on the list than "employee." Reminding myself of that helps me clarify what I should do. Sometimes I can't go home and work takes precedence, but if I'm routinely putting "employee" over "mother," then it highlights to me very early on that something is wrong. Here's another way this works. In the list above, "sister" comes after "author." But I know in my heart that in the great scale of things, my relationship with my brother is way high on this list. Yet I haven't spoken to him for a couple of months and I feel bad about it. I'm prepared to bet, because experience has taught me this, that if I take five minutes to call him today, the writing of this book will go more smoothly. When we're living a life out of balance, life is tougher. When we're clear about what's important and focusing on it, life flows more smoothly.*

14

The perfection trap

Your need to "get it perfect" isn't about perfection. It's about staying in control.

And staying in control is not a virtue if it's making you miserable.

I have a friend who ran her first marathon. And she did run the whole way, never once slowing down to a walk. She felt fabulous for about six hours afterward—she deserved to. Then before she'd even had her evening meal, the self-doubt began— she should have run faster, pushed herself more, achieved a better time. All she'd wanted beforehand was to complete the race but now that she had, she couldn't stop beating herself up for not doing it "better."

When she told me this story, I sat dumbstruck by her perfectionism. She looks better than me, earns more than me, achieves more than me, but the price for her success is a small voice inside telling her endlessly that she's just not good enough. Does it have to be that way? I think perfectionists can achieve just as much if they let that voice go for good. They tend to think not. They know their perfectionism is neurotic but they cling to it because they think they are lazy and that without the voice they would just give up and slouch around the house in old bathrobes, not brushing their teeth.

Here's an idea for you...

Restrict your to-do list to seven items only. Less a to-do list than an I absolutely have to do list. Chinese medics say that any more and you get stressed out by the sheer volume and fed up when you don't complete them.

This is unlikely. However, only you can learn to ignore the little voice. What I do know is that if you don't ignore it, you'll never be free of stress. Often that little voice belongs to someone we know, often someone who brought us up, who has no idea of the complexity of our world. In their world, with one role to fulfill, it was easy to do it perfectly. In the world we live in, chock-full of choice, where we can fulfill so many roles, there's no way we can do all of it perfectly. And even if you did, you still wouldn't be happy. Give it up!

■ Ration your perfectionist behavior. You probably won't ever lose it completely. However, you can limit it. One woman I know whose energy levels had plummeted finally made the connection between her habit of staying up late reading and answering emails and her inability to get to sleep (duh!). So now she allows herself two nights a week to check emails late. Go through your own life figuring out where you can cut down or cut out perfectionist habits.

■ Lose your fear of the person who made you this way. Even if you were always the sort of kid who liked to color code your books, no one becomes a perfectionist unaided. Someone somewhere had high expectations of you. Accept something pretty basic: If you haven't earned their unconditional approval by now, you probably never will. Let it go. And if you can't, get therapy.

■ Walk barefoot in the park. Remember Jane Fonda begging Robert Redford to stop being such a stuffed shirt and to walk barefoot in Central Park? You could try the same—just to see if you like it. You probably won't, but it might teach you something valuable: That nobody cares but you. Whatever your version of mad devil-may-care spontaneity—asking friends to dinner and ordering takeout, or letting your roots show, or putting on a few pounds, or refusing to take the kids swimming on Sunday morning because you simply can't be bothered—go ahead and *do it*. The kids will not implode with disappointment. The world will not fall apart. Slip up and nothing happens.

No one cares if you're perfect but you (and the person who made you this way; see above, but we've dealt with them already).

Perfectionism is often linked to the need to please others. Check out IDEA 3, *Cure yourself of the "disease to please*," for some advice on this.

Try another idea...

"The question should be, is it worth trying to do, not can it be done."
ALLARD LOWENSTEIN, political activist

Defining idea...

61

How did it go?

Q How can I stop the inner voice from nagging me?

A *Think about a mistake you've made recently or something you failed to do. Then hear the voice telling you off. Listen closely. Summon a visual image of the voice. Now draw a picture of your visual image and every time you hear the voice scribble on it, deface it, unleash your destructive tendencies. Externalizing helps. Reject your inner critic. It's rotten company.*

Q I like everything to be nice. I can't function in mess and squalor. I can't sleep if everything isn't done. How can I strike a balance?

A *Why are you reading this? OK, I'll hazard a guess. Everything isn't nice. Everything feels like it's about to pop. A doctor friend of mine once said to me that she saw dozens of women trooping through her office complaining of stress and exhaustion. After a bit of questioning it would emerge that these same women routinely started ironing at 10:30 p.m. and then wondered why they were stressed out and resentful. "It's self-evident that you can't stop being stressed until you stop putting yourself under stress," she said. "There isn't a magic pill that allows you to work sixteen-plus hours a day in one role or another and be a well-rounded, happy person at the same time—otherwise I'd be on it!" You have to make choices. You either let your standards slip a little, or accept that you'll always be stressed.*

15

A shortcut to coping with obstacles

For every behavior or action, there's a payback. When you work out the payback you often drain away a lot of stress from a situation.

OK, this is a brutal one. Don't read the rest if you're feeling fragile. This is where we take the gloves off.

These are some of the random (cruel) thoughts that have crossed my mind during conversations with friends and acquaintances in the last couple of months:

- If you're over thirty-five and still trying to please your mother, it's time you stopped, not least because acting like a child isn't going to advance your chances of ever having a half-decent relationship with her.

- If you're a man (or, indeed, woman) who uses work as an escape route to get out of going home, it's pretty obvious to everyone what's going on, including the folks back home. Maybe that's why your family is so darned unpleasant when you bother to show up.

Here's an idea for you...

Write down three situations in the last week that have stressed you out. (Say, missing the train to work, arguing with your sister, staying late at work.) Then figure out what the payback was. Make a game out of working out the payback for your actions on a daily basis. It's interesting to observe when you're "running a racket" (which is life coach speak for kidding yourself).

- If you're single, over forty, and unhappy about it, then you made choices even if these didn't feel like choices at the time. Your choice was to run from the people who wanted to commit to you in favor of those people who didn't want to commit to you—all of whom, incidentally, you invited into your life.

- If you're a mother in the developed world still breast-feeding a one-year-old child several times a day, you're doing it for reasons of your own that may have little to do with your child's needs and everything to do with your own. The fact that you're exhausted and your relationship with your baby's father is shaky isn't all that surprising.

- If you're feeling awful because you've had an affair, you deserve to. Not for the mindless sex but for neglecting your primary relationship in the first place. You were too cowardly to address the problems and are too cowardly now, having precipitated a crisis instead in order to force your spouse to make decisions.

■ If your child is using explicit swear words to your mother-in-law you probably should feel guilty. Not for giving birth to a delinquent but for being disrespectful to the old bird behind her back, even if she is a pain in the neck, even if it is good fun to laugh at her.

Check out IDEA 18, *How to make everyone love you,* for more on dealing with difficult situations.

Try another idea...

Remember, I didn't actually say these things. These people were distressed and the last thing a distressed person needs is a know-it-all. My friends wanted sympathy and that's what they got. However, if we were really serious about sorting out our stress levels, we could start by taking our share of the responsibility for creating them.

TAKE RESPONSIBILITY

When you realize the great truth that you create a lot of your stress by your choices, then you're in a position to work out the payback—your "reward," what you're getting from the situation. And I guarantee that there will always be a payback. Sometimes the payback is worth the stress. You choose to look after your ill child. Nothing could be more stressful. The payback is, of course, self-evident.

But others are more tricky and take great honesty. Fired from your job? But remember, you decided to stay when the company started

"I think of a hero as someone who understands the degree of responsibility that comes with his freedom."
BOB DYLAN

Defining idea...

65

going downhill because the pay was good and it was near your home. Being chased by the tax man? Hmmm, did you wonder why your tax bill seemed low, but weren't concerned enough to double-check your accountant's figures?

So whatever your stress source, look carefully at what choices of yours led to it: excitement, money, security, perpetual childhood, a sense of competence. You might decide that the payback is worth the stress.

But just by recognizing that in every single thing you do, every single relationship you have, every single habit you've got, you are getting some sort of payback *or you wouldn't do it* is incredibly liberating. Recognizing the payback gives us immense self-awareness. Obstacles melt away because we stop blaming everyone else. Once we're self-aware we tend to change of our own free will. The truth will set you free. Honest.

Q **Are you always this smug?**

How did it go?

A *Sorry. This involves a lot of honesty and quoting real-life situations shows how much is needed. I honestly believe this is one of the most useful life skills you can learn. And I'm still learning it. Today, as I write this, the sale of my apartment has fallen through because the building super won't agree to do some repairs within a short timescale. I wallowed in self-pity for a good half an hour—why is it always so complicated, why is it easy for other people and not me? Blah, blah. But the truth is, my habit of trying to duck confrontation with my super has allowed him to dodge these repairs. So I won't be doing that again. The payback isn't worth the stress.*

Q **I am not getting anything from my stressful situation (nursing my terminally ill mother). What advice do you have to offer me?**

A *This is one of the situations where you can't take any responsibility. Try this technique. Ask yourself "What is my ideal outcome from this?" That doesn't stop you from being realistic about the situation. Your ideal outcome cannot be "Mother gets better." But what would you wish for her? What would you wish for yourself? What does the "ideal you" in this situation look like? When we concentrate on making it as positive an experience as possible despite the heartache, we start to think laterally, productively, creatively for solutions that hadn't occurred to us before.*

16

Stress is other people

Here's how to deal with the energy black holes.

Most of the time I wander through life in an agnostic muddle. And then, occasionally, life flows with such serendipity and I am so in the right place at the right time, that I think there must be a god.

One day I bumped into a woman I knew slightly, a refugee who has gone through more in her twenty-seven years than anyone should have to in a lifetime. She was clearly upset, tears beginning to roll down her cheeks, and I stopped to see if I could help. Here was a woman who had walked stoically through war zones. What the hell had made her so desperate in central London? She told me she had been going through the ticket barriers at Oxford Street subway station but hadn't been able to get her ticket to work the automatic gate. The inspector had started shouting at her, querying if she had paid for her ticket and accusing her of obtaining it illegally. "It has made me feel like giving up," she told me. "I thought maybe it's because he's

Here's an idea for you...

A lot of stress in our relationships with other people come from trying to second-guess what they're thinking or what their intention is. Try saying: "What other people think of me is none of my business." Think about that statement closely. When you start believing it, life gets a whole lot easier.

racist, and I'm black. But then I thought, no, it's me. I'm so stupid and my English isn't good. Total strangers hate me on sight. It's my fault. I'm never going to fit in here." The shame and humiliation had ripped through her already fragile self-esteem and made her doubt if she could ever cope in the UK.

As I listened, my mind was whizzing furiously. My eyes narrowed. "Was he tall, skinny, wearing thick glasses?" I asked her. She nodded. Clearly this wasn't the response she'd been expecting. What she didn't know was that only the week before I'd had a run-in with that very man at the same station. He had picked on me for no apparent reason. So I was able to assure my friend that it wasn't her. It was him. To hear that I—white, native, and with English as my mother tongue—had been similarly abused by this bully changed around her day.

All around you are the energy black holes, people who are unhappy, negative, or angry and who would like nothing more than to drag you into their stressful world. And there is absolutely nothing you can do about them. The only thing you can change is your attitude. (There is a proviso to this—if your life is littered with difficult people out to get you, then with respect I might suggest that it's got something to do with your expectations.) But sometimes, even most times, it's not you—it's them.

SOME BLACK HOLES ARE STRANGERS

Other people have their own agendas. You can't know what they are and you can't change them. Take a tip from Rosamond Richardson, author and yoga teacher. She recommends visualizing yourself surrounded by white light, creating a protective bubble around you. Negativity just bounces off this white light and can't affect you. Sounds nuts, but it works. Try it and see.

While you can't control other people, you can control your day. IDEA 43, *Perfect moments*, has some tips on this.

Try another idea...

SOME OF THEM YOU SHARE A LIFE, A HOME, A BED WITH...

Don't waste a moment dwelling on how less stressful life would be if John would only be kinder, Mom would cheer up a bit, Emily was more help around the home, or your boss was less aggressive.

This is a surprisingly telling little exercise that you can do in five minutes on the back of a napkin. It may shock you. Make a list of the people with whom you have regular contact. Then divide that list into three categories:

■ **The energizers.** They look after you in every way. They give great advice. They bring happiness to your life.

■ **The neutral.** They're OK. Neither great nor bad.

"A healthy male adult bore consumes each year one and a half times his own weight in other people's patience."
JOHN UPDIKE

Defining idea...

71

- **The drainers.** They're users, people who don't deliver, let you down, bring you down. They also include gossips; people whose conversation is sexist or racist and bitchy; sarcastic types whose conversation, no matter how entertaining, makes you feel bad about yourself afterward.

And you know what I'm going to say. Maximize time with the energizers. Look for them when you enter a room and gravitate toward them whether you've been introduced or not. We all know these people when we meet them. If you have too many neutrals, think how you can bring more energizers into your life.

And the drainers? Your time with them should be strictly limited. And if some of them are your closest friends, your family, your lover, you need to think about that very closely. You may feel unable to cut them out now (although that is an option) but you can limit the time they are allowed to suck you into their world.

Q **At work, I'm surrounded by a lot of unpleasant bullies—that's the culture. They complain about me—and everyone else. What can I do?**

How did it go?

A *Do you work hard, step up, do your best? Are you fair and impartial, pleasant as you can be? Yes? Then you're doing all you can. Don't spend time worrying about what they're saying about you. Look for a new job.*

Q **You make it sound easy but it's not. I'm surrounded by unhappy people and they look to me for support. I can't let them down, can I?**

A *Well, if that's what you want. But there's not much chance of you achieving a stress-free life anytime soon. Try to limit the time you spend with them and/or limit their opportunities to talk negatively. When you're not counseling them, do cheerful things. Build up your sense of self. You'll be amazed at how it will affect how other people treat you. They'll either perk up around you, or drop you. And then you will be able to decide what's more important to you—your role as a carer or having a stress-free life.*

17

Watch out for that iceberg!

Like the *Titanic*, you're sailing along and coping like a trooper and then, *kaboom*, you're sunk. You can't get out of bed. That's iceberg stress.

Most of the stress is hidden under the surface, and by the time we realize how bad it is, it's too late.

Although as many as one-third of people admit they have been laid low out of nowhere with some mysterious stress-related illness, I'd suggest respectfully they are being somewhat disingenuous. There are always signs, but we rarely pay attention to them until they are dangerous. It's possible to go on for a long time with low grade stress symptoms. A very long time.

Diane, now forty-two, had a classic case of iceberg stress. Much as I love the self-help movement, eternal optimism in the face of difficulties is not always the appropriate response and it didn't do Diane any favors. She started her own business at thirty-five with big hopes. After three years she was still struggling. "I was massively in debt, working 14 hours a day," she says. "I had no other life but I kept telling myself that all the business geniuses whose books I read avidly had gone through the same

Here's an idea for you...

Write down your ten emotional highs in the last month and ten emotional lows. If it's easy to think of the bad times, but not the good ones, you may be more stressed than you realized. Feeling emotionally defunct is a sign that burnout could be closer than you think.

thing just before their breakthrough and huge success." She was nearly always exhausted, which she put down to gynecological problems and not enough exercise. Her response was to start training for a triathalon. Meanwhile she kept bursting into tears and getting pains in her chest. One day as she was doing laps up and down the swimming pool, she started having what she thought was a heart attack. When she got to her doctor's office, Diane was told she was having a panic attack, hyperventilating so badly that she couldn't breathe. "My doctor finally had to give me a reality check," Diane recalls. "Business success was perhaps just around the corner but I wasn't going to be around to appreciate it. I was cracking up under the stress."

Diane's story illustrates so many aspects of classic iceberg stress—the perfectionism, the desire to take control (triathalon as an answer to exhaustion? Duh!), the belief that if she only worked harder and longer it would all be OK. Her doctor immediately signed Diane off sick for three weeks and she ended up taking six months off in total. She wound up her business, and is now happy working as a manager in a small company where she has all the creative license she wants. She is still paying off the debts accrued during her enforced six-month sabbatical—but she has her life back.

The signs will be there, but are you paying attention? A recent study discovered that 48 percent of people admitted to being irritable because they were stressed, 44 percent didn't sleep, 35 percent were permanently exhausted. But then there were the 19 percent who claimed that stress had no effect on their health at all. They're the true workaholics.

Bad food exacerbates iceberg stress. IDEA 20, *Eat the stress-free way,* has more hints for a healthy lifestyle.

Try another idea...

Below are a few questions worth asking yourself. It will give you an idea of where you fall in the stress gradient, stage 1 being less difficult than stage 3. Those with stage 1 may be showing mild signs of iceberg stress, those with stage 2 moderate symptoms. Exercise, sleep, a decent diet, and—most of all—changing your habits will do a lot to help. Those on stage 3 should consult their doctor and consider overhauling their lifestyle pronto. They almost certainly have iceberg stress.

Stage 1—Snowball
- Do you often get minor skin blemishes such as cold sores?
- Do you get cravings for sweet, sugary foods?
- Do you experience energy slumps?

Stage 2—Snowman
- Are you prone to acne that doesn't appear to be related to puberty or menopause?
- Do you get every bug going and find it hard to recover from illness?

"People who don't know how to keep themselves healthy ought to have the decency to get themselves buried, and not waste time about it."
HENRIK IBSEN

Defining idea...

- Do you get constipation or suffer stomach problems such as bloating or acid reflux?
- Are you inexplicably overweight?
- Have you lost weight because you're just too busy?

Stage 3—The whole iceberg
- Do you suffer from exhaustion all the time?
- Do you suffer from eczema that is getting worse?
- Do you have irritable bowel syndrome that's not under control?
- Do you suffer from high blood pressure, palpitations, or dizziness?

Q   **I have a few pimples, and you're telling me that I'm heading for a heart attack. If there aren't any major symptoms, why take action until you hit stage 3?**

How did it go?

A   *Well, that's one choice. The one most people make. But just as you can function for years with high blood pressure before being stricken by a fatal heart attack, you can function with iceberg stress for years before it has an adverse effect on your health. But the sooner you deal with it, the less damage it will do. If you let yourself be overcome with iceberg stress, it can take months, even years, to come back from it.*

Q   **I know lots of people who are overweight and exhausted. How can you tell when stage 3 is getting serious?**

A   *That's the worst part—you can't tell. How it works, according to stress expert Liz Tucker, is to imagine a cup being filled with a few drops of water at a time. The cup is you, the water is stress. If the cup is regularly emptied (let's call that relaxation), then it doesn't come anywhere near overflowing. If the stress keeps collecting in the cup, nothing happens until the cup is near overflowing, but all it takes is just one drop and then it all spills out. You'll never know what your last drop will be. It won't need to be anything dramatic—a missed train, a bad conversation, that supersize burger and extra fries. Just one stressor too many and that's the ball game. Sunk.*

18

How to make everyone love you

Take the moral high ground. You'll like the view.

We are approval-seeking missiles. From birth we seek the praise and validation of others. And this constant need for approval is the source of some of life's great stresses.

We start off wanting a smile from Mommy for playing nicely or using the potty. And it's a direct line from that to remodeling your house so it's bigger than the neighbors' and stealing your coworker's ideas at work to impress the boss. Unfortunately, success-driven behaviors don't always supply (hopefully) what we got from our parents when we were kids—the praise and the absolute certainty that we are fabulously loveable and important.

A sure way to feel important is to feel superior and the way to do it is to find someone we consider inferior to ourselves and then demonstrate very clearly to them why we're so much better. This is the origin of most success-driven behaviors. Which is why many of us spend much of the time feeling like schmucks—mainly because we spend much of the time behaving like schmucks. Seeking external approval, although a low-risk strategy as a child (if you have a loving carer, you

Here's an idea for you...

For the rest of the day, try treating everyone you meet with exactly the same warmth as you would your best friend. Smile when you see them, compliment them on their appearance, let them know how they are adding to your general well-being. When you answer the phone, smile. Let your thank-yous ring out loudly. Being kind to everyone from the postman to your partner seems to halve stress levels.

nearly always get it), is a high-risk strategy as an adult because it's often based on placing ourselves on some hierarchy of success and (a) there's always someone higher up the ladder than you and (b) there is rarely a captive audience taking the place of your parents and cheering you on. (And that's why we need to grow up and build our own inner reserves of self-esteem, but that's a whole other story.)

When we're still comparing ourselves with other people—what they have, what they do—we feel worth less than them. And that sets up a deep anxiety that is stressful and usually leads to you trying even harder to make other people realize your superiority.

And one day you wake up and no one seems to like you much. Not even your kids. Especially your kids, as they are the people on whom you probably act out your surreptitious "inferiority/attempt-at-superiority" routine more than most. In fact, the success-driven behaviors that we embarked upon to win approval are likely to result in the direct opposite. People think, at best, you're a bit needy and pathetic and, at worse, you're a grade A pain in the backside.

WHAT WOULD NELSON DO?

Here is my favorite trick. The minute I start to feel the stirrings of inferiority— whether it's that my boss is unhappy with me, my partner is fed up with me, friends don't phone anymore, that I'm generally worthless—I stop and think "What would Nelson Mandela do?"

IDEA 28, *Turning Japanese*, might help you to achieve the calm you need to love the world.

Try another idea...

He's my man. But for you it could be Jesus, the Dalai Lama, Oprah Winfrey, Batman. Create the fantasy of them reacting to the situation you're in—and then behave as your hero would.

If somebody appears to think you are worthless, try to figure out what is motivating their behavior. This is not the same as worrying about what they think about you. It's not about you. It's about them. Try to see into their hearts—can you see any worry or stresses that could be motivating them to act mean? Do your best to make them feel better. Remember that all of us are approval-seeking missiles—including the people who are acting out their inferiority/superiority thing on you.

Be a hero in your own life. You will stop feeling the need to act superior to stop you from feeling inferior. You will speak to people straightforwardly, refusing to be intimidated by those you feel are superior to you, declining to play the silly game of putting yourself on some weird pecking order determined by who has the biggest house, best job, bigger salary, more degrees, smarter kids, thinnest thighs.

"We can secure other people's approval, if we do right and try hard; but our own is worth a hundred of it, and no way has been found out of securing that."
MARK TWAIN

Defining idea...

You will be a person walking confidently through life spreading grace and goodwill. You will love the world and it will love you right back.

How did it go? **Q I get so intimidated by people that I come across as cold. What can I do to give a better impression?**

A *Self-consciousness can do that. Here's a tip from life coach Martha Beck: When you're in a situation where you feel intimidated, pretend the other person is a guest in your home and your job is to make them feel comfortable. The hostess scenario creates an equal relationship but at the same time you are so busy making them feel good (that's your part of the contract as hostess) that you forget to feel self-conscious.*

Q Isn't all this higher-self stuff a bit hokey?

A *Yes, but it works. Here's something else that might work. Ask someone you love to identify five positive qualities that you possess. Scan the list and pick one that resonates with you, one you'd like people to attribute to you. You'll find that it worms into your mind and you try to live up to it despite yourself. What other people see as good in you is a powerful motivator. Never underestimate the long-lasting effects of your positive word. Be insincere and you'll come across as an idiot, but genuinely look for the good in people and be authentic in your praise and others will cherish the memory of your kindness for years and that goodwill has to boomerang back on you with good effect some day.*

19

Grumpy old man—or really, really sick?

If you're a man and you're angry, could it be your hormones that are to blame?

There is a school of thought that says men have menopause, too. At some point in midlife their hormones go haywire and that's the reason they turn into miserable old geezers.

Stressful for anyone who has to live with them—and for them, too, one must imagine. Now I'm not saying I go along with this theory, because I've spoken to lots of eminent doctors who say it's so much wishful thinking to excuse men's bad behavior (before you accuse me of man-bashing, all these doctors were male!). However, research into primates shows that corticosteroid hormones released due to stress do indeed lower testosterone. Lower testosterone would seem to be linked to becoming nervous, withdrawn, and to lashing out irrationally. And if that describes you, you'd probably like to think there was a medical explanation so you could let the police know when they come calling later. So, read on.

Here's an idea for you... **Get off the cigarettes and stay off them if possible. If you smoke, you're not helping yourself. Smoking doesn't relax you—in fact, it causes you to get hyped up. (Think what you'd do if you were having a smoke and your boss stormed through the door in a rage with you. No, you wouldn't keep smoking.) Give up but get support. A recent study has discovered that people who were sent encouraging texts from loved ones intermittently throughout the day found it much easier to quit.**

Psychologist Jed Diamond has written a book on this subject, *The Irritable Male Syndrome*. He quotes research he has done into the self-reported psychological state of over 6,000 men. According to Jed, 50 percent are irritable "almost all the time"; 43 percent exhausted "almost all the time"; 46 percent are bored "almost all the time"; and 41 percent of men are "never" sexually satisfied. (Cue mass raising of eyebrows from women all across the land.)

Depression, anger, anxiety, fatigue, moodiness, and low libido—our men are facing a crisis of some sort for whatever the reason, hormonal or otherwise. We women can mock men for trying to jump on our bandwagon and find hormonal reasons for their bad behavior but I do think that the statistics in the paragraph above are probably fairly typical. Increasing pressure to maintain a job given no one has one for life and increasing demands from women to be more equal partners (one in four women marry a younger man, according to the *London Times*, possibly because they have the energy to keep up with them). Whatever. No wonder men are in a constant state of tension.

Life isn't much fun for lots of men as they hit their middle years—and it's not much fun for the people who love them either. What helps?

When you find it hard to talk

Many men aren't great at talking through their feelings. Jed Diamond recommends going for a walk, as men are better at communication when side by side than face to face (oooh, scary!). Or you could try going for a drive. The enclosed space allows for uninterrupted chat, and the lack of eye contact takes the pressure off.

See IDEA 12, *Lost your mojo?*, for more on boredom.

Try another idea...

When you're permanently down

Eventually if you want to stop being irritable, you have to find your way back through rediscovering your passion for life. Let's hope it's not for your secretary. If you're struggling to find a reason to get out of bed in the morning, much less find your passion, start small. The important thing is action. Think of one goal you'd like to achieve that would make you feel good—a small goal is fine. Make a list of what you need to do to achieve it. Start working toward happiness as you would toward any other goal.

When you spend your time glued to the TV

Professor John McKinley, a top researcher into male menopause, is convinced most of the symptoms are due to being overweight, drinking too much, and being inactive. Depression may be in the mix somewhere. TV or any other distracting behaviors are just a way of avoiding the fact that you're mental and physical health are shot. Harsh words. But if you're overweight, try losing ten pounds and doing some exercise—that will help your health and mood immensely.

"Life is full of misery, loneliness, and suffering—and it's all over much too soon."
WOODY ALLEN

Defining idea...

How did
it go?

Q **I've read stories of men who have responded well to testosterone. Is these any truth in these reports?**

A   *Doctors for the most part are doubtful of these hormonal fluctuation theories and think it more likely a ruse to persuade gullible men they need sexy-sounding testosterone therapy—a potentially harmful treatment, as well as being expensive.*

Q **My guy has all the midlife symptoms of geezerhood. But he's only twenty-nine. Is there anything I can do?**

A   *According to psychologist Jed Diamond, this isn't restricted to men in midlife (what we used to call middle age). He doesn't believe that all the symptoms are due to hormonal fluctuations. Some are psychological, too. I do think there is a very good case to say that in the last few decades women have been given more arenas to succeed in—career, wife, mother, "good" person doing worthy things even if it doesn't pay. Men are expected to have multiple roles but don't get as much praise for these as women—all of this on top of their main role as breadwinner. The frustrations can be immense. So be patient.*

20
Eat the stress-free way

Let your diet support you in your battle to de-stress. Lose weight, think clearly, sleep better. All this can be yours with food combining.

This approach to food helps people eat more healthily without too much effort.

Food combining is probably one of the most successful diets of all time. In a nutshell, it advocates never mixing concentrated protein and concentrated starch at the same meal. One group is acid forming, it's claimed, one alkaline. Mixing them puts stress on the digestive system and stops us from reaching optimum health.

Unmitigated nonsense, most doctors will tell you. The digestive system is perfectly capable of coping with steak and fries at the same time. But then there are thousands of people who swear that food combining removes recurrent health problems and helps them think clearly, lose weight effortlessly, and stay calm. I am not going to enter into the scientific arguments but I do think that food combining is an excellent way to improve your level of nourishment and that's got to be good for your stress levels. It's almost impossible to experiment with it even on a part-time basis without improving your diet by about 100 percent. Partly because it's near impossible to eat processed foods and the less processed food you eat, the healthier you get. Good nutrition always helps guard against the damaging effects of stress.

Here's an idea for you...

Try to cut back on alcohol, artificially sweetened food, coffee, tea, soft drinks, margarine-type spreads, and sugary foods and drinks. These all put a strain on the body and you're trying to minimize this.

I felt good when I tried it for two weeks—relaxed and well. If I did have gut problems, I would definitely return to it. It is based on the ideas of Dr. Hay (older versions are known as the Hay Diet) and they can be rather persnickety. However, I recommend the approach taken by nutritionist Kathryn Marsden, who's written several books on the subject. She has done more than any other person to make food combining easy and achievable and, yes, stress-free.

People who are stressed often suffer from upset stomachs. Food combining helps people who suffer from digestive problems because it improves bowel function. It is good even in cases of anxiety-related bowel problems. It can help with pain, bloating, and regularity. Kathryn Marsden reports that irritable bowel syndrome seems to respond particularly well to food combining.

Here are some basic principles. Try one or two—or all of them—and see if they work for you.

- Don't combine concentrated proteins with concentrated starches at the same meal (see next page). Vegetables can be eaten with either protein or starches, as can a small amount of nuts. Fats and oils can be eaten with either. Stick to good-quality ones—organic butter, cold-pressed olive oil.

- Eat fruit only on an empty stomach—several pieces for breakfast, or as a midafternoon snack, or as a starter before a meal. This is because fruit eaten with other foods can contribute to gas and bloating.

- Introduce a small green salad as a starter to your main meal each day.

Read IDEA 32, Is stress making you fat?, for more good dietary habits.

Try another idea...

- Eat dessert or fruit an hour after finishing your meal if at all possible. Sugary foods interfere with stomach acid and affect the transit of the rest of your meal.

- Start slowly. Kathryn Marsden recommends eating one food-combining meal for two days each week and gradually upping the numbers. "If you end up food combining for around five days out of every seven or for two meals out of three, you should gain considerable benefit," she says.

- Don't get too hung up on it. Work in broad categories. It's not the end of the world if you mix a little protein with carbohydrates. Rice, for instance, is predominantly carbohydrate but does contain a little protein. Most foods are a mixture (which is where food-combining critics have a field day). But the idea is to get the big picture and categorize foods according to the main group that they fall into. Nuts can be either protein or carbohydrate but should be eaten in small amounts.

Examples of concentrated proteins
Beef, canned fish, cheese, chicken, eggs, milk, yogurt, fish, game, lamb, liver, pork, shellfish, soybeans.

Examples of concentrated starches
Barley, basmati rice, biscuits, bread, brown rice, bulgur wheat, buns, corn, couscous, flour of all kinds, muesli, oats, pasta, pastry, pita bread, porridge, potatoes, legumes (except soy), sweet potatoes.

"To safeguard one's health at the cost of too strict a diet is a tiresome illness indeed."
FRANÇOIS DE LA ROCHEFOUCAULD

Defining idea...

How did it go?

Q   **So what does a food-combining menu look like?**

A   *You could start the day with oatmeal (made with water, not milk—no protein with starch remember), served with almond, oat, or rice milk and a spoonful of manuka honey (excellent natural sweetener). Or you could have lean bacon, eggs, tomatoes, and mushrooms. Lunch could be a baked potato with a large, crunchy green salad, or vegetable soup with French bread. Dinner? Chicken with grilled vegetables, fish with salad, couscous with stir-fry vegetables. Leaf through a good book on food combining and you'll soon see the food can be far more delicious than I can ever describe it here.*

Q   **Don't you have to be awfully organized?**

A   *Well, yes. It does take more effort until it becomes second nature. Plan your week's menus before you shop. Make a list. If you're not organized you will end up panicking and reaching for a packaged meal. But in some ways, planning what you're going to eat and being organized is stress relieving, too.*

21

Stress-proof your Xmas

Season of goodwill and cheer? Yes, if you're not worn down by the constant partying, endless entertaining, relentless cooking...and let's not start on the shopping.

This year, let's make it different. No hassle, no stress. Honest!

"Dear Santa,

All I want for Christmas is that you transform my family into a perfect one full of sweetness and light, and, most of all, appreciation. Also, despite the fact that I feel pressured into buying enough presents for a small European state, cook a four-course feast, and put up with a drunken father-in-law, let it be stress-free. Oh, and if you could see your way to sprinkling the whole season with magic dust so I get excited because it was a bit of an anticlimax last year, that'd be terrific."

Would your letter to Santa read like this? You wouldn't be alone. One survey discovered that we rate Christmas as one of the most stressful life events, just after moving, changing jobs, and divorce. Two-thirds of us are mentally and physically drained after Christmas.

Here's an idea for you... **Get the worry out of your head and on the page. Buy a beautiful notebook and keep it with you at all times from November on. Scribble down ideas for presents, stray thoughts about the menu, addresses of friends for cards, babysitter numbers...anything you'll need.**

So to avoid "crash and burn," try this countdown. I must have written about fifteen articles over the years on "stress-proofing" Christmas, and this is the crème de la crème of the tips that worked for me.

START EARLY

For me, Christmas cards were always a complete chore, not to say bore. But then I started following the advice of my friend, Kate. "I have an old box covered in Christmas paper and each year I fill it with Christmas cards and stamps. It stays on the kitchen table all through November and I'll sit down most evenings, put on some nice music, pour a huge glass of wine, and get it done." I, too, now have a box and from the middle of November, I do five cards a night. It takes 20 minutes max—including the inevitable calls to check addresses that mysteriously haven't made it into my address book.

THE ONE-DAY SHOPPING BLITZ

I spend one day shopping for my family and one day shopping for everyone else. I have a good idea what I'm buying for my family so it's not too stressful. For everyone else I do it in one day, in one store. To make this fun, go with a friend. Take a day off work and meet in the best department store in town for breakfast. Then at 10 a.m. sharp spend three hours shopping and meet again for lunch in the store's restaurant. Then split up for another two hours and meet up for afternoon coffee. Finally, split up again and meet for cocktails in the bar across the street at 6 p.m. You can adapt this idea to suit yourself and your environment. If you do everything via the internet, allow yourself just one day to do it all. This method focuses the mind. You have to make decisions quickly.

THE CUTOFF POINT

Christmas Eve is magical. I often enjoy it more than Christmas Day. For me Christmas Eve is about missing the last-minute rush. I like to take the day off, build a big log fire, listen to carols on the radio, and heat up some mince pies so the smell wafts through the house. Pretend I'm a domestic goddess for just one day, basically.

But if you have to rush around, or even like to rush around, at least give yourself a cutoff point after which you put down your tools, pour yourself a glass of something bubbly, and take an hour or so to admire your tree piled high with presents. The end point focuses you and, funnily enough, you'll get it done by then.

Try IDEA 26, *Restoration day.* Elements of this are perfect in the countdown to Christmas.

Try another idea...

"Next to a circus, there ain't nothing that packs up and tears out faster than the Christmas spirit."
KIN HUBBARD, humorist

Defining idea...

How did it go?

Q My family loves Christmas but I'm bored with it. How can I get some enthusiasm back?

A *Enjoy tradition, but don't be a martyr to it. Introduce some new elements. Why? Because at the root of our traditions is a desire to re-create the Christmases we remember from the past, but a lot of what makes those memories special is that when we were children, it was all new. We have to open up to being just a little surprised if we want it to stay fun and fresh as well as comforting. Mix it up every year. Serve chinese food. Stagger present opening all through the day rather than having one rip-fest. Go to the early morning service rather than the midnight one. If you don't enjoy an idea, no worries—switch back next year.*

Q My family always ruins Christmas with their behavior. How can I get them to see what they're doing?

A *I think we expect a little too much of Christmas Day. Nowadays, we crowd it with so many of our expectations of perfect family life that no wonder it rarely fulfills our dreams of what it should be. Stress counselor Gladeana McMahon says that we should be clear in advance what behavior we expect. "Say 'I love you very much, I want you here, but I won't put up with…' (fill in the blank). On the day, if you sense things are going wrong, try to divert the crisis. If that doesn't work, you have to call their bluff. Leave the house—yes, even if you're the hostess. Go somewhere else where you can enjoy yourself and take the people that you want. It sounds extreme but sometimes badly behaved people need that shock to realize how badly their behavior is impacting you."*

22

Are you too stressed to be happy?

Stress saps our energy and eventually our enjoyment of life. Stress makes us unhappy without us even realizing it.

Do you accept the stressed-out state as just the way you are? Does it have to be this way?

Are you healthy? Hopefully, you'd answer "yes" immediately. But if I told you that the World Health Organization's definition of good health is not just an absence of disease but the "presence of *emotional* and physical well-being" (my italics), you might hesitate. Few of us can remember when we last felt 100 percent emotionally and physically well. And the chances are that it's stress that's bringing you down.

One of the most pernicious things about stress is that we start to think the stressed state is "just life." We forget there was ever a time when we didn't get upset by the neighbors or feel guilty about how little we've achieved. These questions are geared to help you pinpoint how stress is affecting your well-being, perhaps without you realizing it.

Imagine what it would be like to live without irritation and self-blame? Recognizing these emotions as being the product of stress is the first step toward emotional well-being.

Here's an idea for you... **Lemon balm helps beat anxiety and irritability. You can buy lemon balm herb in supplement form at your pharmacy or find a supplier on the Web.**

Stage 1

Do you have a sense of injustice or resentment against people you don't know such as big lottery winners or acquaintances who seem to have a much better life than you?

Do you say "should," "ought to," "must" a lot?

Are minor issues with neighbors or colleagues dominating your thinking?

Stage 2

Do you feel guilty about being unhappy with your life?

Do you find it hard to motivate yourself?

Do you feel tired all the time?

Do you lack confidence and self-esteem?

Stage 3

Have you had repeated problems for a prolonged period of time?

Do you have trouble remembering the last time you really laughed out loud?

Are the people around you a constant source of disappointment?

Do you think that life could be so much better if you could only resolve one negative issue?

Do you suffer from constant anxiety?

Do you think it is impossible to improve your situation?

If you checked any statements in stage 1, you'll benefit from finding more pleasure in the life you've got—seeking out good feelings like a pleasure-seeking missile will make a huge difference to your state of mind.

If you checked any in stage 2, stress is having a serious effect on your mood and could be pushing you into depression. Read on, but consider talking to your doctor.

If you checked any in stage 3, it's time to consult your doctor. You might benefit from counseling.

Mind-sets can change. If yours is a negative one, IDEA 44, *Out of your head*, can help.

Try another idea...

When repetitive thought patterns or overwhelming anxiety are making life miserable, you might want to consider a form of therapy known as CBT (cognitive behavioral therapy), which is designed to work in a matter of weeks. The therapist helps you explore and recognize thought patterns that are holding you back. CBT works on changing the way a person thinks about himself and how he fits in the world. These thoughts usually operate at the edge of a person's awareness and are often molded in childhood. Once you have "named" such thoughts, you can consciously change your thought patterns so that you begin to see the world through a different filter.

Whatever stage you're at, a very good place to start is by making your well-being a top priority. I've met many people who have suffered from emotional ill-health and one recurring theme when they talk about getting back to health is the importance of keeping it simple. They say that if they can just exercise a little, eat well, and sleep at night, it helps immensely, even if they don't believe it will. Exercise and fresh air tires you out so you sleep. Brisk exercise three times a week for thirty minutes has been proven to be as effective as drug treatment in treating depression and only 8 percent of people who exercised became depressed again, whereas 38 percent "relapsed" in the drug treatment group. Keeping to the same hours as the rest of the world means you don't get into the vicious cycle of living "out of sync," which only heightens isolation even more.

"Health is not simply the absence of sickness."
HANNAH GREEN, writer

Defining idea...

How did it go?

Q **I'm on stage 3. I'm skeptical about counseling. Can you convince me this will help?**

A *As a quick exercise complete the following sentences without thinking about them. Give your instant responses. Write them down.*
I am...
Life is...
So I...
What do you have in front of you? Dismal responses? Dire outlook. You'll learn a lot about your view of life from this. With a negative worldview, you are setting yourself up to be stressed for the foreseeable future. I can't pretend that CBT always works, but isn't it worth a try? Look at your responses again. What happens if you do nothing? Trying something new might not work. But it's unlikely that you'll start to feel better if you don't do something.

Q **I am depressed, but I don't know why. My life isn't any more stressed than anyone else's. What's wrong with me?**

A *This isn't a competition. There is much we don't know about depression. We don't know why some people get it and some don't. We don't know why some people respond to medical treatment and some don't. There are few illnesses that are more stressful. It tends to overwhelm everything and worst of all makes it difficult for people to do anything to help themselves—no control, major stressor! Sometimes people are too depressed to even go to the kitchen and turn on the teakettle. Please recognize that beating yourself up isn't doing you or anyone else any good.*

23

Purge your home in a weekend

De-cluttering. Space clearing. Majorly de-stressing.

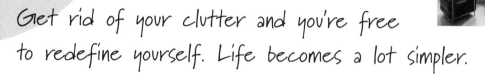

Get rid of your clutter and you're free to redefine yourself. Life becomes a lot simpler.

Everything I own fits pretty neatly into the average living room—and that includes my car. I started de-cluttering about ten years ago, and I haven't stopped since. It's addictive, it's life affirming. Nothing makes you feel so serene and in control of your life as chucking out stuff you don't need.

Smug? You bet. Life wasn't always this way. For all of my twenties and most of my thirties I had all the furniture, plants, ornaments, designer clothes, and bad taste costume jewelry you'd expect of someone who reached adulthood in the '80s. Then in the early '90s I thought I'd write about this new gimmick I'd heard rumors about—feng shui (remember that!). And that's how I ended up inviting space clearer Karen Kingston into my less than fragrant home. She told me to clear out the closet, clean out the junk under my bed, and get rid of my books—"let new knowledge in." Then the magic started to happen.

Here's an
idea for
you...

Try the "one in, one out" rule. For instance, if you buy a new pair of shoes, then you must get rid of an existing pair. An added bonus is that this system protects you against impulse purchases of stuff you're not really excited about, as you have to focus your mind on what you'll throw out when you get home.

Life picked up a pace. In the three years following my meeting with Karen, I moved out of the home I'd lived in for years, traveled extensively, and reorganized my working life so I earned enough from working half the hours.

My job is to research and write about what is called self-help, or "mind, body, or spirit." I've done it all from meditation to colonic irrigation. But nothing transformed my life like de-cluttering, or to give it its esoteric name, space clearing.

THROW IT OUT, LOSE THE GUILT

How does it work? Most of us live among piles of ancient magazines, defunct utensils, clothes that neither fit nor suit us. The Chinese believe that all these unlovely, unwanted things lying about haphazardly block the flow of energy—the chi—in our homes. My theory is that by losing them, we lose a ton of guilt—guilt that we'll never fit into those hellishly expensive designer jeans again, guilt that we spent all that money on skis when we only go skiing once a decade, guilt that we never cook those fabulous dinners in those two dozen cookbooks. You get my point. Just about everything in your home probably engenders some sort of guilt. Cut your belongings by 90 percent and you do the same to your guilt.

THE BIG CLEAR OUT

"Useful or beautiful, useful or beautiful"—
that's the mantra. If any single object doesn't
fulfill one of these criteria, trash it. Cultivate
ruthlessness. If you haven't worn it, used it, or thought about it in a year, do you
really need it?

Have three trash bags on hand as you work. One for stuff to throw out, one for stuff
to give to charity, one for things you want to clean or mend. Visit the secondhand
shop as soon as you can—make it a priority. Give yourself two weeks to tackle the
"mend or clean" bag.

Something neither useful nor beautiful, but that you don't want to get rid of for
sentimental reasons? Put it away for a year. Time out of sight makes it easier to get
rid of.

Do this little but often. Try a couple of one-hour sessions per week. I operate the 40–20
rule: 40 minutes cleaning followed by 20 minutes sitting around feeling virtuous. You
get better at de-cluttering. Soon it's second
nature. Do two to three sessions a month.

Find a home for everything you own. You're
allowed one drawer that acts as a "junk drawer"
for all the odd items.

Once you've started de-cluttering you're ready for the master class in IDEA 25, Hug your home.

Try another idea...

"If more of us valued food and cheer and song above hoarded gold, it would be a merrier world."
J.R.R. TOLKIEN

Defining idea...

103

How did it go?

Q   I would de-clutter but most of the mess in our home is due to the children. How can I get them to be a bit tidier?

A   *I have instigated the "scan" into our family life. Just before we leave for school and just before our kids go to bed they "scan" each public room and tidy up their detritus. Also be aware that it's really difficult for children to keep stuff tidy if they have too much of it. Regularly cull their toys and books of anything they haven't looked at in six months. When they're little, do this while they're out, keep the bag for a month, and if they notice anything is missing, surreptitiously return it to their belongings. If they haven't missed it within a month, give it to charity. As they get older, children can enjoy doing this for themselves. They feel they're being generous and it teaches them the importance of recycling.*

Q   But this stuff is expensive. How can I just get rid of it?

A   *I know it's hard, but that is fear talking. Fear that if you give away that $400 suit that you've worn twice, you'll never get another one. But it's that very suit hanging in your wardrobe reproaching you that stops you from looking around for something that would suit you better. Get rid of the suit, and a better one will take its place—one that you might possibly wear. Or something else will happen. You'll change—you'll end up with a lifestyle that only calls for jeans and the suit will be redundant. Have faith.*

24

The stress clinic is open

You know you're stressed and you know it's affecting your health. Here's what to do about it.

Stress hits your hormones hard. And this can make its effects felt in the darnedest places.

IF YOUR DIGESTIVE SYSTEM IS UPSET

Adrenaline slows digestion so food hangs around in your gut for longer, leading to constipation and bloating. Conversely, noradrenaline acts to open up the bowel, which leads to diarrhea. That's one reason why irritable bowel syndrome (IBS), which is often stress-related, can manifest itself with apparently opposite symptoms.

Take action: Probiotic supplements boost the good bacteria in the gut and this will help combat the effects of the stress hormones. If IBS is a problem for you, there has been some progress in the last few years. You might find your doctor more sympathetic than previously and now able to offer you different treatments.

Here's an idea for you...

Make a list of your top seven people. Think of how important your continued good health is to them. If you can't do it for yourself, concern for those you love can be a powerful motivation.

IF YOUR SKIN IS PRONE TO ACNE OR VERY DRY

When you're stressed, your body diverts resources away from areas that don't contribute to its immediate survival—that means your skin. Stress also makes women produce more testosterone and that can lead to a breakout of acne at times of stress.

Take action: A multivitamin will help fill the gap in your nutritional needs, and if your skin is dry take a balanced omega 3 and 6 oil (try Udo's Oil from health food shops). If acne is the problem, your doctor can prescribe drugs that will help.

IF YOU GET HEADACHES

Adrenaline is one of a group of chemicals known as "amines" and people who get migraines are particularly sensitive to them.

Take action: The Migraine Association recommends that those who get migraines avoid another amine—tyramine. This is present in foods such as caffeine, chocolate, cheese, and red wine. Eat these on top of the effects of stress and you are serving up a double whammy.

IF YOU'RE ALWAYS TIRED

The hormones that regulate sleep include serotonin and melatonin—and both can be affected by periods of stress. Research has found that this is compounded in people who don't sleep particularly well. They have high levels of the stress hormone cortisol— which unsurprisingly keeps you alert. Not useful at bedtime.

Take action: People who are short of sleep get into a hopeless cycle, thinking nothing works. This can be a self-fulfilling prophecy. To be honest, it is hard to sleep when you're right in the middle of a stressful period—your doctor may be able to help with a short-term prescription. Sleeping pills, if only taken for a very short period at a time of crisis, are not addictive, but should only be taken for a few days. What is more worrying is when after the period of stress is over, you still have trouble sleeping. Then you need to tackle the problem aggressively.

Read about the Alexander technique in IDEA 31, *Standing tall*. It can ease all sorts of physical distress as well as relax you.

Try another idea...

IF YOU'RE PRONE TO WEIGHT GAIN

We're learning more all the time about stress and one thing we've found out in the last decade is that there's a link between stress and weight gain. Stress is thought to interfere with the action of insulin, which regulates energy release. This could be contributing to a condition known as insulin resistance, which leads to weight gain along with an increased likelihood of other dangerous conditions such as diabetes.

"On the plus side, death is one of the few things that can be done just as easily lying down."
WOODY ALLEN

Defining idea...

Take action: Dieting won't necessarily help with insulin resistance. A low-calorie diet per se won't help the problem much if you are still eating the kind of carbohydrates that cause big fluctuations in insulin release, mainly processed ones. What will help is limiting the carbohydrates that you do eat to healthy ones such as vegetables. Have some fruit and whole grain bread and pasta—but don't overdo even these, healthy though they are. Stick to one or two servings of them a day and eat them with a little protein or fat, such as a few nuts or some yogurt with a piece of fruit or some cheese with your toast. This slows the breakdown and thus insulin release into your bloodstream.

Ultimately, getting on top of stress will help with all these problems. If you are suffering health symptoms that you know are related to stress, it's more important for you than most to look for solutions that will help you.

Q **I have terrible IBS. My doctor's been no help. Are there any alternative approaches you can suggest?**

How did it go?

A *Some people have discovered that symptoms improved when they cut out various foods to which they appear to be allergic. This is controversial, but if you're desperate, it might be worth trying. Hypnotherapy has also worked well for some people, though no one quite knows why.*

Q **I suspect I have insulin resistance because, despite not eating much, I keep putting on weight. What do I do?**

A *You can read more in* Syndrome X *by Leslie Kenton. Check out* The South Beach Diet *by Dr. Arthur Agatston for a good, practical eating regime. But basically avoid processed carbohydrate foods, which include bread, pasta, rice, cakes, cookies. Watch out for potatoes and fruit, both of which trigger the same sort of insulin release that you get from eating processed carbohydrates. Stick to vegetables, meat, fish, and a little low-fat dairy for a week or two, but read more in the books I've just recommended if you're going to do this for longer.*

25

Hug your home

It's hard to feel unstressed when your home a mess. And even if it's clean, keeping it that way is often a major cause of stress.

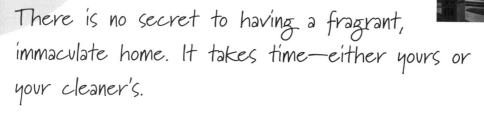

There is no secret to having a fragrant, immaculate home. It takes time—either yours or your cleaner's.

But even if you have a cleaner, at the end of the day we all have to do a bit of cleaning—unless you've got the luxury of a 24/7 housekeeper.

So here are some ideas for making housework stress a thing of the past. It will benefit two groups of people:

- The owner of a messy home—your house will be cleaner.

- The owner of an already immaculate home, but the price for it is you find yourself cleaning the kitchen stove at midnight. Believe it or not, you can benefit, too, but you can skip through the first part snorting with derision.

Here's an idea for you... **When cooking, fill the sink with hot, soapy water and dump stuff in as you go along. Yes, even if you have a dishwasher. It helps you keep surfaces clear and then you enjoy yourself more, too.**

I am not a slob, but neither am I a perfectionist. So given that I'm busy, domesticity is way down on my priority list and my house gets dirty—certainly far below the standards acceptable to my grandmother. It used to upset me until I found www.flylady.net. I urge anyone domestically challenged to seek it out. A bit hokey, but sweet, it's a support group for those who have felt overwhelmed by the ceaseless round of domestic duty and fed up struggling with it alone. They have rules. One of them is that the minute you get up, you make your bed, get dressed (including shoes), wash your face, and get your makeup on, and/or shave. Try this and you'll be amazed at how much more productive you are. I have adapted some of their other rules to suit me. (Hint: The first tip here changed my life.)

ALWAYS HAVE A CLEAN KITCHEN SINK

With a shiny sink, you feel you're in control. Wash dishes by hand if necessary (yes, shocking, but it's a skill you haven't forgotten). A shiny sink reflects back a vision of yourself as a domestic goddess (or god) in stunning control of your world. Don't leave home or go to bed for the evening without clearing the sink area. It really is best to clear your kitchen right after the evening meal—or get your kids to do it. Before bed you can't always be bothered and it sets the morning off to a bad start.

ADOPT THE LASER BEAM APPROACH

Divide your home into clearly defined areas.
You will clean one of these areas thoroughly
every week. No area should take more than an
hour. This could look like: hallway and bathroom; kitchen; reception rooms;
bedroom and spare bedroom; children's bedroom(s). Now make a list of what you
need to do to each area to get it cleaned to your satisfaction. Keep a master list for
each room in a file. The reason for this? With a list you get to check off items and
that's immensely satisfying. First thing Saturday morning is a good time to clean,
not least because if you have children they can get involved.

BLESS YOUR HOME

The FlyLady website calls it the Weekly Home Blessing hour—and this is the
superficial cleaning you do to keep your home bearable. It takes an hour a week—
or you can split it up. I do ten minutes morning and evening, three times a week
That on top of the hour a week I spend on one area is usually enough to keep my
(small) home bearable. You may have a larger home and need to put more time in.
During my ten-minute sessions I do one of these activities: sweep and mop floors;
vacuum; dust; clean bathroom; polish all reflective surfaces; get rid of all trash—
purge magazines, empty contents of recycling bins.

**No point cleaning a lot of old
rubbish. IDEA 23, *Purge your
home in a weekend*, will
inspire you to de-clutter.**

Try another idea...

**"At the worst, a house unkept
cannot be so distressing as a
life unlived."**
ROSE MACAULEY, writer

Defining idea...

How did
it go?

Q   Why on earth do I need a file?

A   *For the slackers and the perfectionists. Slackers: Checking things off on lists makes you feel in control. And it means you actually do it rather than procrastinating. It is worth getting up ten minutes earlier to feel that your home is a fragrant, happy zone. Perfectionists: Limit yourself to this amount of cleaning—use the time saved to relax and put into action some other de-stressing activities.*

Q   Why not just get a cleaner?

A   *Having a cleaner whose standards are lower than your own (pretty lax) ones doesn't help—and it's amazing how many people are in that boat. At the end of the day, you have to do some cleaning yourself. The best advice I've received on cleaners is to make sure they clean and you tidy. I don't have a cleaner now but I took the view when I did that it wasn't her job to unload the dishwasher. You want your cleaner to be prioritizing the cupboards you haven't seen inside for decades and getting into the corners you're always too busy to do. Paying your cleaner to pick up your kids' toys probably isn't the best use of her time and your money.*

26

Restoration day

When you're suffering from chronic, long-term stress. When your batteries are blown. When burnout is imminent, here is your emergency plan.

Book yourself a day out. By tomorrow, you will feel rested, stronger, and more in control. (No, don't stop reading—you can make this happen.)

All you need is 24 hours. If you have children, ask someone else to look after them for as much of the day as possible. Remember that if you don't look after yourself, you will have nothing left to give to others.

The restoration day is based on three principles:

■ Replenishing your body by giving it rest.

■ Resting your brain by focusing on your body.

■ Nourishing your soul with healthy simple food that will replenish the nutrients stripped away by stress.

Here's an idea for you...

Go to bed at 9:30 p.m. today and every day this week if you can manage it. Don't watch TV if you're not tired–read or listen to music. People who do this have turned around their stress levels in a week.

Before you get up

When you wake, acknowledge that this day will be different. Today you are going to shift the emphasis onto relaxation and releasing tension and replacing what stress has drained away from your body. Stretch. If you feel like it, turn over and go back to sleep. If not, read an inspirational tome—a self-help book, poetry, a favorite novel. Don't reach for your usual coffee or tea; sip a mug of hot water with lemon. This, according to naturopaths, boosts the liver, which has to work incredibly hard processing all the junk that goes into your body. Whatever, it's soothing. Every time panic hits because you're not doing anything—now and for the rest of the day—breathe in deeply for a count of eight and out for a count of eight.

When you get up

Stretch for ten minutes. A few yoga stretches are good, but it doesn't matter as long as you try to stretch every muscle in your body. You don't have to do this "perfectly." It's not a workout, it's a reminder—you have a body, it carries tension and pain. Feel the cricks draining out. Finish with the yoga position known as the Child's Pose. Kneel with your legs tucked under you. Bend forward so your forehead rests as near to the floor as possible in front of you. A cushion on your knees might make this more comfortable. Take your arms behind you with hands pointing back and palms upward. Rest like this and breathe deeply. This is a favorite of mine because it releases tension in the neck and shoulders, which is where I store tension. I've been known to climb under my desk at work and do this for a few moments.

Breakfast

Try a fruit smoothie. Blend a cup of natural yogurt with one banana and a couple of handfuls of other fruits; peach, mango, strawberries, pineapple. Thin, if preferred, with a little fruit juice. Sip slowly, preferably outside. Imagine the vitamin C zooming around your body replacing the levels depleted by stress. My advice today is to eat lightly and avoid (except for the odd treat) foods that strain digestion too much. Drink coffee and tea if you normally do; the last thing you want is a caffeine withdrawal headache. But don't have more than, say, three caffeinated drinks. Caffeine will make you jittery even if you're very used to it.

Look at IDEA 43, *Perfect moments*, and incorporate those ideas into your rest day for an even more chilled-out experience.

Try another idea...

Morning

Get outside, in the most natural surroundings you can manage. Ideally, lie on your back on the grass. Stare at the sky. Let your mind drift off. Or walk in the countryside, the park, sit in your garden. If you really can't bear to be still, do some gardening.

Lunch

Have a huge salad combining every color of vegetable you can think of—green, yellow, orange, purple, red. More vitamin C. Serve with a delicious dressing. This meal must include one absolute treat—a glass of wine, a dish of ice cream, a piece of chocolate. Lie back. Indulge.

"Rest as soon as there is pain."
HIPPOCRATES

Defining idea...

Afternoon

Go back to bed or curl up on a cozy corner of your sofa. Watch a favorite movie or a comedy show. A tear-jerker can be great for this. A good cry is very therapeutic. Sleep if you can. Or if you'd prefer, listen to some favorite music.

Dinner

You should be hungry but feeling light. Eat another pile of vegetables—a salad or perhaps a stir-fry, following the "eat a rainbow" advice given above. Have a fresh piece of fish grilled or fried in a little oil or butter. Think delicious but simple. Present your food beautifully; eat it by candlelight.

Go to bed early. Resist the temptation to watch TV. Read a book, listen to the radio or some music.

Q **Can't I just stay in bed?**

A *Better than nothing but it won't relax you as much as following a structured program. The restoration day looks deceptively simple but it works on a deeper level. I've lain in bed all day when I've been stressed and I've done this—this works much much better.*

Q **What about exercising?**

A *Formalize the stretches by going to a yoga class if you really must, but although exercising is terrific for stress, it's not part of the restoration day because it brings a competitive everyday vibe. Today should feel like a vacation from your usual schedule—a change really is as good as a rest. I suggest taking a day off work rather than doing this on the weekend. Knowing everyone else is working doubles the efficacy!*

How did it go?

27

Crisis management

Facing the week from hell? Here's how to survive it.

This is the toolbox for navigating through those really stressful, busy times.

DON'T CATASTROPHIZE

Dorothy Parker, on hearing a telephone ring, apparently drawled "What fresh hell is this?" We've all been there. On really busy days with multiple deadlines, I've gotten to the stage where I'm scared to answer the phone in case it's someone demanding something else of me. Then I made a conscious decision to stop being such a victim. My attitude became "Why fear the worst until it happens?" Every time a negative thought crosses your brain, cancel it out with a positive one. This takes practice. An easy way to do it is to develop a mantra to suit whatever crisis you're in today and that you say to yourself automatically every time your mind goes into tailspin. Right now, I have to pick the kids up from school in half an hour. I have four weeks to my deadline for this book and I have done approximately half the number of words I promised myself I'd write today. My mantra is "I am serenely gliding toward my deadline and everything will get done" and every time panic hits, I chant this to myself and feel much better.

Here's an idea for you...

Keep a time log of your working week so you finally get a realistic idea of how long it takes you to complete all your usual activities. This means you stop kidding yourself about how quickly you will perform tasks in an imperfect world where you're interrupted frequently, and you'll reduce your stress levels hugely.

MASTER THE ONLY QUESTION THAT MATTERS

The "best use" question was taught to me by my first boss and it is invaluable in negotiating your way through any day with dozens of demands on your time. It helps you to prioritize "on the run," sometimes quite ruthlessly. On the morning of manic days decide what you have to achieve that day and if anything interrupts, ask yourself, "Is this the best use of my time right now?" If the answer is no, take a rain check and come back to it later. So if a friend calls at work, nine times out of ten, you won't chat then, you'll call her back at a more convenient time—unless, of course, she is very upset about something. Then talking to her *is* the best use of your time. Nothing else is more important. By doing this, I don't let colleagues sidetrack me with complaints about their lack of stationery, unless of course it's the best use of my time. (No, you're right, so far stationery has never been the best use of my time, but you get the idea.)

ALWAYS UNDERPROMISE

A lot of stress is of our own making. Thomas Leonard, who founded Coach University, the first professional training center for life coaches, says, "One of the biggest mistakes is to tell people what they want to hear, give them what they think they want, without thinking if it's feasible for you. You overpromise results you can't deliver without a lot of stress. And of course, if you don't deliver, not only are you stressed, *they* are, too." Leonard's advice is to underpromise rather than overpromise. That way your friends are delighted when you show up at the party you said you couldn't make and your boss thinks you're wonderful when you get the report finished a day early rather than a week late. Make it your rule from now on to be absolutely realistic about how long it's going to take you to get things done. And until you get expert at this, work out the time you figure it will take you to complete any task and multiply it by 1.5.

When you've got tons to do, use this in conjunction with the rotation method explained in IDEA 4, *Never procrastinate again*.

Try another idea...

"There cannot be a crisis next week. My schedule is already full."
HENRY KISSINGER

Defining idea...

123

How did
it go?

Q **I've tried the mantra thing but it didn't do much good. What did I do wrong?**

A *Did you say it out loud? Every couple of hours, repeat your mantra out loud three times. Remember, you don't have to believe this for it to work. Keep persevering. Perhaps your mantra was wrong. The important thing about "positive affirmations"—which is what we're working with here—is to make them in the present tense. Avoid ones like "I will get on top of my filing": This implies you will always be about to get on top of your filing, and never actually succeed. I also think it helps to include a word like "serene" or "calm" or "abundant" or "sparkling"—words that lift you emotionally—just for the hell of it. Finally, when time is short and you don't have the time to come up with a mantra, here is my all-purpose one that I find useful on multiple occasions: "There is a way, and I have found it."*

28

Turning Japanese

Learn from Zen. The Japanese bath and tea ceremonies are as much about refreshing the mind and spirit as nourishing and cleansing the body.

Try this and you'll see why the Japanese consider taking a bath to be a sacred experience.

This is my version of the Japanese bath and I try to make time for it once a week, midweek, on a "school night." It works better than a simple candlelit bath. I think that's because you have to put a (minimal) amount of effort in and that makes you feel you're taking back control. The Japanese bath has cumulative effects—the more often you do it, the more powerfully it works. There is a set pattern to it and the predictability is soothing in itself.

You will need: a balancing essential oil such as lavender or geranium or frankincense, an aromatherapy burner, a quiet place to sit, a clean bathroom (free of clutter), some soft towels (preferably warmed), a loofah or a body brush or sisal glove, a small bowl, comfortable clothes, a teapot, a cup, a strainer, loose-leaf tea, a candle, a blanket, and a minimum of one hour.

Here's an idea for you... **Invest in some special props that you keep purely for restoration. The sense of specialness helps turn a bath into an event and with time you will be able to trigger relaxation with just part of the ritual. A cup of tea, a bath with the balancing oil, or body brushing will in themselves be almost as good as the whole ritual.**

First, light the burner in the bathroom, lock the door, and sit there quietly breathing in the fragrance, letting your mind quieten and be still. Lay your hands on your stomach, breathe in deeply, and feel your stomach move out. Breathe out and feel your stomach contracting. Let go of all other thoughts. Now, and for the rest of this hour, keep your focus on what you can see, feel, hear, and smell. Anxious thoughts will intrude, of course. When they do, imagine them drifting off in the fragrance rising from the burner.

When you're relaxed, undress and gently draw a brush or loofah over your body, working always toward the heart. Then step into the shower—it works best if it is at a slightly cooler temperature than usual. Lather up and get really clean. Concentrate on the noise of the shower. Let anxious thoughts disappear down the drain with the soapy water.

Clean? Now step out of the shower and run yourself a hot bath. Add a few drops of your balancing oil to the rushing water. Sink into the bath. When intrusive worrying thoughts interrupt, let them gently float away in the steam. When you're good and chilled out use the small bowl to ladle water all over your body. The idea is not to get clean but to focus your mind on pouring the water as gracefully as possible. Study the pattern of the falling water. Let yourself enter a sort of trance state, soothed by the repetitive actions. When thoughts of the outside world intrude, imagine them moving from your mind to being plastered on your body, and then visualize them being swept away by the falling water.

The Zen approach also works well in IDEA 26, *Restoration day.*

Try another idea...

When your mind is calm and you feel centered, emerge, wrap yourself in warm towels, dry off, and dress in warm, comfortable clothing.

Hold this "mindful" state. Go to a peaceful corner of your home and light a candle. (If you can do this whole ritual by candlelight, it will be even more restful.) Then make some tea, concentrating fully on every step. Watch the kettle boil, relax and breathe deeply, and keep your mind as restful as possible. Concentrate on the candlelight if it helps. Make your movements as graceful and economical as possible.

Green tea gives the authentic Eastern feeling. Herbal is best, but any tea will do. Finally, retire to your quiet place, cozy up with a blanket, sip your tea, inhale the fragrance, focus on the candle flame, keep your attention on it. Concentrate on the taste of the tea. Imagine anxious thoughts drifting away in the fragrant steam rising from your cup.

"There must be quite a few things a hot bath won't cure, but I don't know any of them."
SYLVIA PLATH

Defining idea...

How did it go?

Q I couldn't switch my mind off. Any tips?

A   *This is a form of meditation and that never comes easily. Try to concentrate fully on what your senses are delivering to you at any one moment. Of course, worrisome thoughts will intrude but with practice you get better and better at dismissing them.*

Q I find it hard to visualize my problems drifting away. Could you explain how I should go about this?

A   *Some people find it helps to see their thoughts passing like a parade in front of them. Others see them written down as a ticker tape. Another method is to see each of your worries as a concrete image with a label stuck on it that "names" it. Sometimes our minds work so fast that we don't even stop long enough to name those anxieties passing through our heads—they just become a blur of general anxiety. Practice this and you'll slow down that ceaseless twittering of anxious thoughts, what the Chinese call "monkey chatter."*

Q I'm just not a bath person. Will a shower do?

A   *The principle is one of ritual, repetition, and calm. You can take the key components of this bath and apply them to just about any situation—a ritual shower if you prefer, or one night a week when you always go to bed early. The important thing is to follow the same pattern of actions and to keep this time sacred to you. You can enjoy a ritual milk shake, if that's what lights your candle—it doesn't matter as long as you do it in a state of mindfulness with the intention of giving yourself a breathing space.*

29

Make like Tigger—learn to bounce

Everyone gets stressed. Everyone gets disappointed. But how come some people are better at dealing with it than others?

The answer is that they're natural "bouncers." But you don't have to be born that way.

Disappointment does one of two things: It makes you "bouncy" (resilient) or it makes you "bitter"—and which one you end up is a more telling predictor of future happiness than rich or poor, nice or nasty.

Bounceability is easy in your twenties. Underneath the veneer of sophistication most twentysomethings are teenagers at heart convinced that their life is going to be fabulous. But during our thirties, the decisions we make pretty well determine what sort of person we're going to be, and how we decide to deal with setbacks is one of the greatest determinants.

According to psychologist Dr. Al Siebert, bouncers exhibit flexibility. "If you look at someone who doesn't handle life well," he writes, "it's often because they think, feel, or act in only one way and can't see any alternative." That means they get stuck in

Here's an idea for you... **Next time you're in the middle of a crisis, try to laugh every chance you can. And if you can't laugh, cry. One way or another vent your emotions. Your mind will work better when strong feelings aren't interfering with your ability to think straight.**

an idea of the sort of person they have to be, the sort of job they were meant to do, the sort of partner that's right for them, the sort of life that they "deserve."

I saw a documentary recently about the aftereffects of Black Monday, the catastrophic plummet of the stock market in October 1987. Brokers who had lost everything were interviewed. Nearly all of them had gone off and made another fortune in a business that suited them better. Clearly, these entrepreneurs didn't give up on the dream of being successful but they didn't assume there was only one route, that they had to drive a certain car, live a certain lifestyle. The most successful of all had been on unemployment for a year while he licked his wounds. He'd been wiped out but he used it as a learning experience and then went off to become a multi-millionaire in another field.

Each of us is born, apparently, with a happiness set point that is genetically influenced, but crucially, not fixed. We can come from a long line of grumpy bastards but at the end of the day our genes only seem to account for about half of our propensity for happiness—or unhappiness, depending on how you look at it. However, what we learn from grumpy parents is likely to be a lot more influential than what we inherit. We learn that life is fixed, that we can't change, that we're not in control. But that's wrong. The thing to remember is this: Your brain chemistry is not fixed. You can change it.

How? When bad stuff happens, ask yourself what are known as "coping" questions, which challenge inflexible thinking. What would be useful for me to do right now? What is the reality and what is merely my fantasy about this situation? Can I salvage anything from this?

Then ask yourself some "serendipity" questions. Why is it good that this has happened? What am I learning from this? What could I do to turn this situation around?

Ultimately, what it comes down to is remembering that everything changes and change itself is the source of stress. Bad stuff happens to good people. But there are plenty of people who have had every disappointment in the book and still lived useful, happy lives. And before you mutter "good for them," science will tell you that there's no reason why you can't be one of the bouncers, too.

Looking after yourself physically is a basic of bouncing. IDEA 20, *Eat the stress-free way*, is a good place to start.

Try another idea...

"Hope begins in the dark. The stubborn hope that if you just show up and try to do the right thing the dawn will come. You wait and watch and work. You don't give up."
ANNE LAMOTT, writer

Defining idea...

How did
it go?

Q   **I'm in a terrible situation and it's very difficult not to get bitter. What do you do in the middle of a crisis?**

A   *You take control. A study that looked at plane crash survivors found they have lower levels of anxiety and stress when flying than frequent fliers who have never gone through a crash. What's more, those who had taken initiative during the crash—helped others to an exit or shared oxygen—had the healthiest psychological profiles of all. Studies of some homeless people in Calcutta found them to be happier than rich Californians because they have such a tremendous sense of community (this sounds fatuous but is nevertheless true). Vent your emotions, pick yourself up, do something to help yourself, and if you can't think of anything, do something to help someone else. Control. That's the essence of bounce.*

Q   **What if I don't have the energy?**

A   *There is a certain element of acting here—and for good reasons. The research shows that acting happy actually changes your physiology and makes you feel better. But it's not simply whistling in the dark. Don't deny your bad feelings, but don't allow yourself to sink into them. Recognize that everyone goes through these feelings. Bouncers don't let themselves get overwhelmed, that's all. Observe your feelings from a distance. See them as interesting and transitory. Another thing you could try is to pick up the phone and make your peace with someone who's done you wrong. Forgiveness is strongly linked to happiness. Read more about turning around your mind-set in the work of Martin Seligman, the godfather of "positive psychology."*

30

Zap those piles

We're talking about the avalanche of paper, magazines, unpaid bills, flyers for pizza parlors—the general detritus of twenty-first-century life that threatens to overwhelm you.

Not to mention your kitchen surfaces.

This idea is very personal to me. Following it has reduced stress in my life by a factor of ten. When my daughter, then three, was asked what her mother did for a living she said "My mommy tears bits of paper out of newspapers." Which is actually quite an accurate description of what I do for a living—it's called "research." I spend hours tearing out, but it's never enough. All my working life, piles of paper have dragged down my spirit and proven to be a stressor in my domestic life. My partner objects to hefting piles of magazines off chairs before he can sit down.

This is the system that works for me, culled from reading and interviewing just about every organizational guru on the planet. The only drawback is that it takes time to set up. But if you have a day to spend or ten free hours, give it a try. Ten hours can work magic. You will probably have to make a few adjustments to suit your life.

Here's an idea for you...

Throw out files regularly: It's a good way to keep on top of paperwork. Every time you open a file, put a pencil mark on the corner of it. At the end of six months or a year, you'll be able to see in a moment which files you've barely opened. Most of their contents can be chucked out.

STEP 1

Gather together everything that you will need to create order in your world. For me that's cardboard magazine holders, folders, pens, labels, stapler, a couple of hard-backed address books (personal and business), and a huge industrial-strength trash bag. I also keep the family calendar and my planner on hand so I can put dates directly into them as I reveal the invites and school dates in my pile.

STEP 2

Work systematically. You are going to go from one side of your desk to the other, or one side of the room to the other. Gather together one pile of paper and assorted junk and place it right in the middle of the room or your desk. Start sorting. Every single piece of paper that you touch must be actioned.

- If it contains a phone number that you might need in the future, then put the number straight into one of your *address books*.

- If it is a bill that has to be paid, or anything that must be acted on immediately, then create a file for *urgent and unpaid bills*. (I carry this file with me, in my handbag and work through it every day when I have a down moment.)

- If it is an article or piece of information that you might need in the future but that is not urgent, start creating files for these (*named files*) such as "investments," "vacations," "general interest."

Read more about why your piles are stressing you out in IDEA 23, *Purge your home in a weekend.*

Try another idea...

- If it is a piece of information that you need to act on or read or make a decision on but not now, put it in a file marked *To Do* and make an appointment in your planner sometime in the next week when you'll deal with it. This file should be somewhere accessible and you should clear it not less than once every two weeks or it gets out of control.

Keep a *tickle book*. Tickle as in "tickle my memory." Mine is a hardbacked notebook. In it I note down the names of anything I might need in the future: the idea of an article I might write or a savings account offering a good rate of interest. The point is that I don't have to hold on to endless scraps of paper just in case I ever want this information—there's enough in the tickle book to help me trace it. I also keep the tickle book by my side at work and if anyone calls me with a piece of information I may need but don't know for sure, then I scribble down their number and a couple of explanatory lines so that I can follow up later. Same with my emails. The tickle book means I have been able to throw out dozens of pieces of paper almost as soon as they reach my desk.

"We can lick gravity but sometimes the paperwork is overwhelming."
WERNER VON BRAUN, rocket engineer

Defining idea...

How did it go?

Q **I can clear piles but I can't maintain order because of the sheer volume of reading matter I'm supposed to get through to be on top of my field. How can I keep the paper under control?**

A *Don't read business magazines or journals cover to cover. Scan the contents and choose three articles that seem most important. Tear them out. Trash the rest. Carry the articles with you in your briefcase and read them in your downtime. I don't let my pile of magazines reach more than eight. That's the mystical number. I find if the pile gets above ten, it takes on a life of its own and it takes weeks, even months, to get rid of.*

Q **How long should I keep my bank statements and the like in my files?**

A *As a rule, you should keep bank statements and credit card statements for two years. Anything to do with taxes for seven years. Most importantly in these days of identity theft, shred your statements. Don't just throw them in the trash. Finding that some nefarious type is living it up in Rio on your credit card would be a major stressor!*

31

Standing tall

If your stomach hangs so low there's a chance of it keeping your knees warm, it's time for the Alexander technique.

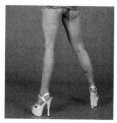

It has something to teach all of us about how we walk through the world.

Every family has its little joke and in my family, I'm it—"little" and "joke" rolled into one. I'm not that small but from childhood my posture has been terrible. I slump, I slouch, I droop, I stoop. In a family of tall people it was inevitable that my nickname would be Dwarf.

Which is why I came to try the Alexander technique. There are two routes to perfect posture. If you see someone with gazelle-like grace chances are he or she is a dancer or a practitioner of the Alexander technique. F. M. Alexander was an actor who was nearly forced to give up his profession because his voice wouldn't behave. He developed his techniques to help him continue projecting.

The Alexander technique is a complementary therapy that quite literally leaves you walking tall. By working on your posture you enjoy a wealth of other health benefits—an end to back problems and less stress for starters. Those who practice

Here's an idea for you...

Feeling tense? Think of your head as floating from your neck like a balloon on a string. Imagining your head as light helps you to lengthen your neck and lift your head away from your shoulders, automatically dispersing tension in the neck and shoulders.

the Alexander technique appear to grow taller, leaner, and younger. Noel Kingsley, the teacher I visited, also believes that by improving our posture we gain charisma, people take us more seriously, and confidence levels soar.

The Alexander technique is so gentle it's quite difficult to know what is happening. A huge part of it is learning to hold our head in a relaxed way. The average head weighs about 11 pounds. Put five bags of sugar in a bag and try lifting it. Exactly. No wonder so many of us feel, literally, that we're carrying a huge weight on our shoulders.

What the Alexander technique aims to teach us is something we once knew instinctively. Look at the perfectly arched back of your children and the heartbreaking grace with which they move—that's what you're aiming for.

The mantra Noel taught me was: "Relax. Float. Lengthen. Broaden." Imagine your neck relaxing, your head floating, your spine lengthening, and your shoulders and chest opening and broadening. Just repeating the words as you walk along helps.

DE-STRESS—LIE DOWN

This exercise is one used by most Alexander technique teachers as a means to help release tension. As you do it remember the point is to allow your body to lengthen and widen. It helps to have this image in your head.

Lie down on your back on a rug or carpet for 10 minutes with your head resting on 2–3 inches of books and your knees bent so that your feet are on the floor but drawn up toward you. Your feet should be apart, to about the width of your shoulders. Rest your relaxed hands on your stomach. Imagine sinking down into the floor so that you feel tension draining from your back muscles. Let your shoulders release and "melt" down into the floor. When you feel you've got the hang of this, tell your head to float away from your shoulders and feel your spine lengthen. Make no effort. Just use your mind and let gravity and your body weight do the job.

Noel says that doing this daily will help calm you and leave you centered (as well as improving your posture immensely).

Perfect posture helps you to breathe better and to walk gracefully and serenely through life. And when you're 2 inches taller (yes, I "grew" 2 inches after doing the Alexander technique), life is far less stressful.

Other therapies that can help you relax are explained in IDEA 47, *Cherish yourself*.

Try another idea...

"Over the years, your body becomes a walking autobiography telling friends and strangers alike of the minor and major stresses of your life."
MARILYN FERGUSON, writer

Defining idea...

How did it go?

Q   I liked the exercise. What now?

A   The best way of learning the Alexander technique is to visit a teacher. In the United States, look for someone with the qualification ACAT. Or you could try reading Noel Kingsley's Perfect Poise, Perfect Life, *which has lots of handy stress-reducing tips.*

Q   How long does the Alexander technique take to work?

A   I felt better after the first lesson, but it usually takes about six to twelve lessons to really make a difference. The Alexander technique can help you even if you only do it in a very superficial way. That's because it makes you more aware of your body and where and when you're holding tension in your body. Just becoming aware of this can make you less stressed. Here's an exercise recommended by Noel in his book that I find works great when I'm stressed. (He recommends it when preparing for a presentation or interview.) Stand upright and "think" your head free and floating from your neck. Breathe out through your nose and empty your lungs. When you have let the air out as much as you can, release the tension around your ribs to allow the air to come in naturally. Do not suck air in. Breathe normally for two breaths, then repeat the whole process again. Noel warns to stop if you feel dizzy. You shouldn't breathe this way routinely. Just when you want to calm down fast.

32

Is stress making you fat?

Any sort of stress can lead to weight gain.

Stress causes your body to release cortisol and this stimulates the fat-storing hormone insulin. Insulin causes your body to hold on to its fat stores.

And that's if you're eating what you always ate. The trouble is that you might be sabotaging yourself without realizing it. When we're stressed there's a tendency to overeat, especially carbohydrates. (It's not called comfort food for nothing.) That's because carbohydrates cause the brain to release serotonin and this is one of the feel-good hormones that raise mood. In a way, it's a form of self-medication.

As is booze. Terrific at relaxing you. Fabulous for adding layers of fat around your waistline.

STAY SVELTE EVEN WHEN STRESSED

It's not what you eat it's when you eat it.

Researchers discovered that when women ate whenever they wanted they ate 120 calories a day more than those women who ate three meals and three snacks a day at set times. Decide on your meal times and stick to them. No grazing.

Here's an idea for you...

When you're stressed and feel the temptation to reach for comfort food, try sucking on half a teaspoon of honey instead (manuka honey from New Zealand is especially beneficial). Honey causes the brain to release the feel-good hormone serotonin almost immediately. You might find that just that tiny amount will satisfy you and prevent you from pigging out on a bar of chocolate or a bag of cookies, which also cause serotonin release but pack a lot more calories.

Make a conscious effort to cut out salt

We can feel more drawn to salty foods when we're stressed. There could be a physiological reason for this. Salt raises blood pressure and that in turn actually raises cortisol levels—which might have been an advantage when we only got stressed once a month but is redundant for the most part now. Wean yourself from adding salt to food and aim to eat no more than 6 grams of salt a day in processed food. If the levels are given in sodium, then multiply by 2.5 to get the grams of salt.

Get into green tea

Caffeine raises levels of stress hormones and makes you even more stressed. Try green tea. It has about half the caffeine of coffee and a little less than black tea. And it's good for your brain and your circulation as well as your waistline. There's another advantage. A recent Japanese study found that people drinking green tea lost 5.3 pounds after three months, while those who drank black tea lost only 2.9 pounds. It's also thought that chemicals called catechins found in green tea trigger weight loss.

Savor food

Apparently, it takes 20 minutes for our
stomach to register that we've started to eat
and switch off the feeling of hunger. It's
certainly borne out by a small US study of
women who were instructed to eat slowly, chewing each mouthful carefully,
savoring their food. These women were told to stop eating when their most recent
bite didn't taste as good as the first. They lost 8 pounds. In the same period of time,
the control group gained 3 pounds. Our bodies know when we've had enough if we
slow down long enough to listen.

Relax

One study showed that women who made a conscious effort to relax lost an average
of 10 pounds in 18 months without consciously dieting. The truth is you need to
actively relax in order to switch off the stress hormones that could be contributing
to weight gain.

Compete with yourself

The best possible antidote to stress *and* weight
gain is to exercise. Buy a pedometer from a
sports shop. Measure how many steps you take
in an average day (most people average around
4,000), and then do a few more steps each day
until you reach 10,000.

Combine these ideas with a
healthy way of eating, as
described in IDEA 20, Eat the
stress-free way.

Try
another
idea...

"My doctor told me to stop
having intimate dinners for
four, unless there are three
other people."
ORSON WELLES

Defining
idea...

How did it go?

Q   **I've got more than 10 pounds to lose. Green tea isn't going to cut it. Any suggestions?**

A   *Look at the South Beach Diet, created by Dr. Arthur Agatston, who developed his diet to help his heart patients, not to make a fast buck (although he must be pretty glad he did). This is the most successful diet I've come across and works for people who don't "do" diets (including my mother, who has lost tons of middle-age spread and returned to the svelte figure of her youth with this diet). The basic principle is a hybrid of the glycemic index (GI) diet and Atkins (but healthy). You cut out carbohydrates for the first two weeks—no bread, pasta, sugar, fruit—and no booze. You eat meat, fish, eggs, cheese, and vegetables. After two weeks you start reintroducing a few "good" carbohydrates, notably fruit, and a glass or two of wine (he's a cardiologist and he's big on red wine). But the good thing is that cravings for the carbohydrate foods that most experts think contribute to weight gain if we eat them in excess diminish rapidly. Weight comes off easily.*

Q   **I've tried your ideas. I'm eating healthily. I'm still gaining weight. What else can I try?**

A   *How are you sleeping? If you're not sleeping well, you need to look at that, too. Doctors are only beginning to understand the connection between stress and sleep patterns. Several recent studies have found a link between obesity and sleeping fewer hours than average. It's counterintuitive: One would think those that are awake longer would be burning off calories like crazy, but it's not the case. Several other studies indicate much the same outcome. This research is in its infancy, but if you are sleeping badly, accept that it might be affecting your metabolism.*

33

Embrace the dark side

Think you're not an angry person?

Maybe that's why you're so stressed.

I have all the anger of wet flannel. But do I get bitchy? Yes. Defensive? Yes. Huffy? Yes. Go to parties, down a bottle of wine, and start a fight with some hapless stranger because I don't like his shirt? Ooh, yes.

Displaced anger isn't so much a problem with me as a vocation.

And, of course, I'm not alone. There are an awful lot of us displacing our anger into other emotions. That's because we don't like anger in our culture. We don't like it at all. The reason we don't like it is that we're never taught how to acknowledge it, deal with it, use it. If we're brought up well we're taught to suppress it. If we're brought up badly we're taught that it's all right to scream at others' bad driving. The first route makes us feel virtuous. The second route makes us feel victorious. Both routes lead to mucho stress.

It's kind of obvious why screaming at people and being an antisocial creep is stressful. In its extreme form you end up in jail. But why does suppressing anger make us stressed?

Here's an idea for you... **When you're upset, go to a quiet place and have a good groan. Big theatrical groans help to dissipate stress.**

According to psychiatrist Theodore Rubin, people attempt to feel only those feelings that fit in with their view of themselves. But by doing this they put their emotions in a deep freeze; they lose their capacity to feel all emotions as acutely and they run the risk of living half a life.

This made sense to me when I read it. By the time you reach middle age there are a whole bunch of people you meet who only seem half there. They're usually awfully nice. Or sometimes they're awfully vague, but they don't appear to be really "with us." After reading what psychologists have to say about anger, I began to wonder if they are the ones who, by suppressing what's known in pop psychology as their dark side, are suppressing a whole lot of other emotions. They don't take a lot of pleasure in anything very much. They don't really connect with their families, they are ciphers to others. That's stressful for everyone.

Anger is as valid as any other emotion, says Rubin. And it's one we suffer from a lot. Psychiatrists believe we get angry every time we're hurt or let down, but those of us for whom anger is a no-no learn to pervert the anger into another emotion and it becomes anxiety, bitterness, or depression.

Once I went to an anger workshop to "find" my anger. The leader was a tiny red-haired woman. She told us that anger has to be expressed both physically and verbally. She stood in front of a large beanbag (it could have been a bed or a pile of pillows). She held a plastic baseball bat in her hands. She centered herself in front of the beanbag, brought the bat above her head, and *thwack!* She banged the hell out of the beanbag. She did it again and again. "It's best to focus on the person you're angry with," she said calmly. "Imagine they are the beanbag."

Read more about hidden sources of stress in IDEA 17, *Watch out for that iceberg!*

Try another idea...

That scared me. A lot. "But you can't hit a person you're angry with," I squeaked. "It's not a person. It's a beanbag," she explained patiently as to an idiot child. And of course, she's right. The anger is out and nobody gets hurt.

The idea is to thump and bellow your rage on the down swing. It takes practice. If you find it hard to find your voice, just concentrate on developing a rhythm. Let the feelings come in their own time. And they will. If you do this when you're angry, you'll defuse stress in a matter of minutes. You won't be such a nice person, but life will be a lot more straightforward. Once you start bashing out your anger, life gets a lot more fun. For one thing, men with ugly shirts don't have to be scared any longer.

"Depression is nothing but anger without enthusiasm."
STEVEN WRIGHT, comedian

Defining idea...

How did it go?

Q I see what you're saying, but I just don't get angry. I always see the other person's point of view. How can I get mad?

A *Try drawing your anger. Get a big piece of paper and some poster paints. Shut your eyes, visualize hard. Imagine what your anger would look like. Draw. I've done this exercise with others and it's interesting. Some people draw a hard little nut. Others a Vesuvius like lava flow. I drew a black puddle. Well, it would have been black, but someone else was using the black paint and I didn't like to disturb them, so it ended up green. Whoa, what was that? I didn't respect my anger enough to stand up for it and get it the right color even. It was a pretty graphic representation of how I pretended things were OK when they weren't. Draw your anger every week for a month and I guarantee you'll learn something interesting about yourself.*

Q Hitting a beanbag with a bat is the most embarrassing idea I've ever read. Why should I do this?

A *Look, the baseball bat thing works. But if you just can't bring yourself to do it, get the bigger picture which is recognizing when you're angry—every time it happens—and acting to dissipate it. That's the important step that we so often miss. Refuse to burn anger out and you start telling yourself little stories to make yourself feel better instead. And before you know it you're living half a life and 100 percent lies. On the other hand, recognizing your anger, trailing it back to its source, and getting down and dirty with it means you stay in touch with what you're really feeling. As long as no one else gets hurt, that's really healthy. It allows you to be an authentic person. It lets you move on from hurts and disappointments.*

34

Love your money

And it will love you right back. When that happens life gets a whole lot less stressful.

Quickly, without thinking too much about it, write down three phrases that come into your head when you think about your finances.

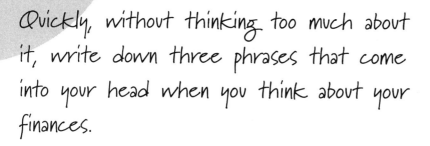

(Hint: Unless your three words are "abundant, balanced, life-enhancing," then you need this idea.)

This idea is about respect. If you're disrespectful of your money, I'm prepared to bet that money is a stressor in your life. If you don't take care of your money, the chances are that, just like a neglected teenager, it's never going to amount to much. Worse, the relationship will probably deteriorate further. One day your money is going to do the equivalent of coming home pregnant with a crack cocaine habit.

Here's a quick test
Get out your wallet or purse. Check out how it looks. Is it neat with bills folded, receipts tucked away? Or is everything stuffed in willy-nilly?

Here's an idea for you...

Go treasure hunting. Look for money in the sofa cushions, in pockets, in foreign currency. How much money do you have stuffed in books? Or unrealized in gift cards? How much of your money are you ignoring?

Here's a quicker one

How much money do you have in your wallet right now? If you're out by more than the price of a coffee, you need this idea badly. Your money is your friend. You should love it like a member of the family. You wouldn't go to the store and forget to bring home one of the kids. Well, why the hell would you misplace your money?

LOOK FOR YOUR LATTE FACTOR

Make a list of everything you spend in a day. Keep a notebook with you and write down how often you take money out and what you spend it on. Every check you write. Every card you swipe. Every time you spend a penny. Literally. Keep it up for a week, preferably for a month. Now multiply (by 52 or 12). That's what it costs to run your life. Go through and highlight the big essentials—the mortgage, the necessary bills. Now get out a calculator and figure out what you spend on lunches, clothes, magazines, newspapers.

You're looking for what has been called "the latte factor," those items that are completely expendable and add very little to your life but cost a fortune. It will frighten the bejeezus out of you. My latte factor was $472. I needed that money a whole lot more than Starbucks. You also realize how much it costs to run your life. The very first day I practiced this exercise I spent $197.45. All I came home with was a pound of cherries. The rest was debt I couldn't remember accruing. Shocking.

We're not going to talk about debt here but if you've got personal debt, do this for a month and you are going to find out exactly why.

If you've got debt, turn to IDEA 37, *Ditch the debt*, for some ways to get back into the black.

Try another idea...

Writing down what you spend is a fantastically useful exercise whether you're overspending or not. It sure as hell won't de-stress you in the short term but it will in the long term. It allows you to see almost instantly who or what you're spending your money on and then decide if you're happy with that. It allows you to take control, and every way you can find to foster the illusion of control is helpful if you want to be less stressed. Spiritual teachers tell us that money is neither bad nor good, it's simply a way we register our presence on the world. If you fritter away money as a distraction, you'll never focus long enough to figure out what's really important to you. If you spend what you don't have, your spirit as well as your bank balance is going to be overstretched. Your bank balance isn't important. Your spirit is. Respect it, protect it, and you're going to make someone very happy—and that someone isn't your bank manager.

"The safest way to double your money is to fold it over and put it in your pocket."
KIN HUBBARD, humorist

Defining idea...

153

How did it go?

Q **I just cannot bear to do this. All you're doing is talking about saving money. Is it necessary to be so persnickety and mean?**

A *If you hate this idea, I'm prepared to bet the whole "disrespecting yourself" theme is pushing your buttons—you're overweight, or you live on junk food, or you lie to yourself about relationships, or you lie to other people about relationships. I don't want to come off all spiritual, but money talks— specifically, what your money is saying speaks volumes about you. What's so scary about knowing where your money goes?*

Q **I've done this, but it's really boring. How can I make it more interesting?**

A *Knowing what you spend your money on is like holding up a mirror to how you are in the world. I'm not saying don't buy a round in the bar. I'm just saying be aware that you currently spend on average "X" a week buying a round in the bar. Knowing that allows you to decide if you're happy with the situation or whether you need to be looking for a new place to drink or, indeed, new friends. When I started writing down what I spent, I lost a vast amount of weight. Was there a subconscious connection between thinking twice before I bought what I didn't really need, and thinking twice before eating food that I didn't really want? Bet your booty. Stuff happens after you start writing down what you spend. And not all of it predictable.*

154

35

End "stop and collapse" syndrome

Take vacations. You know how important this is if you want to be stress-free.

And then you spend the first week in bed recovering from some dreaded illness. You've got leisure sickness—aka "stop and collapse" syndrome.

The guy who first identified leisure sickness was a sufferer. Professor Ad Vingerhoets of Tilburg University noticed he always got ill on the first days of his vacation. So he did a study of nearly 2,000 men and women aged between sixteen and eighty-seven. And guess what? He wasn't alone. A small but significant number of his subjects regularly got ill on the weekend or on vacation. (I think his numbers must be an underestimate because most of the people I know are affected.) He discovered that those who got leisure sickness complained mainly of headaches, migraine, fatigue, muscular pains, nausea, colds, and flu (especially common when going on vacation).

Those who got it shared certain characteristics: a high workload, perfectionism, eagerness to achieve, an overdeveloped sense of responsibility to their work—all of which make it difficult to switch off.

Here's an idea for you... **If you're prone to weekend sickness, try exercising on a Friday evening. Exercise is a stressor but one your body loves. This acts as a transition between work and time off, and helps you unwind quicker.**

One theory is that those who work hard simply get so bored on vacation that they start to notice the symptoms they've been suppressing while at work. It could also be a case of mind over matter: we don't allow ourselves to get sick until the work is done. Yet another theory is that when you're working (stressed) your immune system is actually working better than it does when you're relaxing. When you relax, the immune system slows down, your defenses relax, and *kaboom!*, you're calling the concierge for a doctor.

So what can you do about it? I'm going to suggest a two-pronged attack.

1. Support your local immune system

As a very bare minimum, eat at least five fruits and vegetables a day and take a good-quality multivitamin and mineral supplement. If you drink too much alcohol or are a smoker, you also need more vitamin C, so supplement that, too. I'm also a fan of echinacea, so try that as well (but read the instructions carefully—if you take it for too long, it loses its effectiveness).

2. Plan for vacations with military precision

You really need to gradually begin to wind down in the two weeks before you go.

Cue hollow laughter. You think I don't understand, but I do. In August 1998, the day before my vacation, I worked in the office from 6 a.m. until 11 p.m., went home, packed, slept for three hours, went back to the office at 4 a.m., worked until 8:30, and took a cab straight to the airport to get on a plane. That's not smart. That's borderline lunacy. So let's have no more of the workaholic nuttiness.

Here are some ideas (I am assuming everyone in your household has a valid passport. Young children's passports don't last as long as adults. Not sure about this? Go and check right now. This one small action could save you loads of stress down the line.)

Turn to IDEA 49, *Supplementary benefits*, for more ways to help your immune system.

Try another idea...

Three weeks before you go: Make a packing list. Write down everything you need to take with you and then allocate each lunchtime this week for completing any errands.

Two weeks before you go: Figure out work. Take a look at all your projects and decide at what stage you want to pass them over. Set goals with each project and allocate deadlines for reaching them, preferably all to be tied up the day before your last day.

One week before you go: Start packing. Put out your bags or suitcases in a spare room if you've got one and start the washing and ironing nightmare during the weekend before you go. Do a little packing each night. Also start winding up projects and writing up your notes to whichever colleague is taking over your responsibilities. You can always amend them on the last day if you get further with a project than you planned to. Amending is a lot better than starting them at 8:30 p.m. on your last day.

"Those who don't take the time to be well eventually have to find the time to be ill."
ANONYMOUS

Defining idea...

157

How did
it go?

Q   I'm sick all year-round. What should I do?

A   *People who successfully overcome leisure sickness often do this by making a major change of attitude or change of lifestyle. The operative word here is "change." I'm going to say it again: You have to change. The symptoms of stress can be ignored or suppressed but eventually if you don't pay attention to what your body's telling you, you're going to get very sick indeed.*

Q   I simply can't switch off and that's why I get ill. When I'm away I'm constantly in touch with the office. How can I let go?

A   *Well, I heard of a woman who always vacationed several time zones away from her office to discourage phone calls. "They can never bother to figure out the five hours forward or back thing," she says. But that's no use if you call the office. I could write reams about this, but it's quite simple really. Switching off means just that—phones, emails, texts, laptops. If you're a boss who can't trust your staff to get along without you, that's bad. Cognitive behavioral therapy could help. If you're an employee whose boss is so controlling he's calling you on vacation, that's worse. Talk to him. Or look for a new job.*

36

Too stressed to sleep?

Facts: The most reliable predictor of depression is insomnia. Sleeping less than six hours a night is linked to increased obesity. Sleeping less than seven hours a night is linked to increased mortality.

Depressed, fat, dead. You've got to figure this sleep thing out.

BASICS

If you have trouble sleeping, it's worth reiterating that insomnia is like losing weight. It's not enough to know what to do, you have to act on it. Chronic insomniacs often stay up half the night drinking tea or alcohol, smoking, watching movies. And then they go to bed and listen to the radio and read until finally about 4 a.m. they doze off. If you don't sleep well here are some key strategies:

- Don't drink caffeine for at least six hours before bedtime.

- Eschew alcohol and cigarettes for at least four hours before bedtime.

- Don't look at any sort of screen for three hours before bedtime.

- Get outside every day and do some exercise.

Here's an idea for you...

Try a "power nap" for increased evening productivity. But if you're worried about feeling groggy when you wake, try drinking strong coffee, then nap. It takes at least 30 minutes for the caffeine to kick in, which gives you 30 minutes to doze.

I've spent a lot of time with seriously depressed people and they seem to get out of sync with the rest of us—sleeping during the day and staying up all night. Depressed people who exercise moderately start to feel better and I'm sure part of it is because they begin to sleep the same sort of hours as the rest of us. Keep up all of the above for three weeks.

IF THIS DOESN'T WORK...

Then the best advice is to think of yourself as a little child. Infants are not born with the ability to soothe themselves to sleep, they need to learn it. You will have to re-learn the skill. You need consistency. A cast-iron routine that never wavers.

Stop all chores and any form of work at least two hours before bedtime. Develop a wind-down routine that starts about an hour before bed. Gentle yoga is great for this, or you could lie on the sofa and listen to quiet music. Then run a hot bath. The bath is important. To counteract the heat, your body lowers its temperature. Lowered body temperature triggers sleep. For that reason your bedroom and bed should verge on the cool. Cozy down in bed and read a book that isn't too thrilling and requires a little effort—Shakespeare's good, I find. Jane Austen is soothing. Do this every single night for a week.

IF THIS DOESN'T WORK...

IDEA 45, *Aromatherapy master class*, is a good place to turn to next for help on sleeping.

Try another idea...

OK, let's get radical. You cannot sleep. You either can't get off to sleep or you wake early but you spend an inordinate amount of time tossing and turning. So don't. Just get up and do something else. See your insomnia as a gift. It's the chance to improve your life, to carve out some time for yourself. And before you dismiss this as wishful thinking, a friend of mine recommended this tip to me (she read it in a self-help book) and within four months, it revolutionized her life. Julie used to go to bed at 11 p.m., wake at 4-ish and then lay awake until the alarm went off at 7 a.m., feeling miserable. So she started setting the alarm for 4:30 and getting up then instead. After a few days she discovered her optimal time was 5:30 a.m. She'd have a cup of tea, she'd plan her day. She'd do a little work ("Really impressed the clients when they got emails sent at 6:15"). A sleep expert advised her that sleeping only six hours a night wouldn't do her any harm at all if she got a nap—humans are designed that way. Admittedly the nap is easier for her, as she works at home, but as she says, "You can always take a nap in your car—there's usually somewhere to go." Friends scoffed. Her husband worried. But since she started sleeping less, she's much more relaxed and happy.

'"Nice guys finish last, but we get to sleep in."
EVAN DAVIS, writer

Defining idea...

How did it go?

Q   I can sleep but I just never get the opportunity. We have a young baby and I'm chronically stressed at work. What can I do?

A   *Here's an idea passed on to me by someone who had exactly your problem. Set aside a weekend and do nothing but sleep. Go to bed on Friday night and don't get up until Monday. It helps to be in your own bed, but it's not essential. Don't get up except to take a bath, brush your teeth, and go to the bathroom. Occasionally munch on some toast—nothing too heavy. Have a novel on hand. All this takes organization. You have to call in favors. You may have to promise to hold the fort while your partner gets their chance at a similar "sleep infusion." But the truth is if you're motivated enough, you can make this happen.*

Q   I'm trying your idea of getting up when I wake but I'm spending the time doing chores. It's lengthened my working day. Is this a bad habit to have acquired?

A   *Well, that's OK if you work for yourself. Take time off in the afternoon to rest and recuperate. Get dressed. Lolling around in PJs will make you waste time. Clothes give you purpose. And have a clear idea of a "depth" activity that you want to undertake that will bring meaning to your mornings and your life—yoga, writing a novel, watching every episode of Friends.*

37

Ditch the debt

Live on less than you earn. Hey, radical concept.

As I write this, press reports warn that there has been a sharp rise in people declaring themselves bankrupt. The stress caused by credit or, to call it by its old-fashioned name, debt, is well documented.

And if you've tried to remove the source of your debt you might well be even more stressed. Consolidating credit card debts into personal loans (at a lower interest rate) sounds like a good idea but financial coach Simone Gnesson has reservations. "Lots of clients have done this but it only makes matters worse if you continue spending and don't deal with the original habits that got you into debt in the first place." (Hint: Building up two debts is *not* the way to go.)

You've read it a million times before but here it is again. Get rid of credit card debt. There is no fast fix. It may well take you years.

Here's an idea for you...

Decide on an amount that you are allowed to spend each day. If by any chance you have any money left at the end of the day, stick it in jar and save it. This, too, can become a bit of a game.

Think about hiring a financial coach. The Internet is a good place to look for one of these. You pay a flat fee to them and they'll help you sort through your attitudes toward money and change habits if necessary. If things have gotten desperate, you might need full-on debt counseling.

Move all your debt to a single credit card or two with 0 percent interest (and remember, these 0 percent deals may not be around forever so don't think you can rely on them indefinitely to make the cost of your debt negligible). Check out the Saturday newspaper financial supplements for details on the best current deals. If you have a lot of debt, you will have to do this many times. Find out when your grace period ends, and mark in your planner a month before you start paying interest. Start looking for a new deal then. Allow at least two weeks for the application to be processed and the transfers to be made, although internet banks are usually faster. Make sure you write to the old company canceling your agreement and cut up the card.

Never have more than one credit card for emergencies. Hide this in your house. Some people wrap it in a bag and put it in a freezer. Do not carry it with you routinely.

Pay more than the minimum toward your debt. Aiming for double the minimum is a good rule of thumb. Believe it or not, you can start to enjoy the process—it can become a game, seeing how much you can pay off each month from money you save elsewhere. Try to pay off a little more each month.

HOW DO YOU SAVE MORE MONEY?

Just writing down what you spend is enough to save money usually. But if you need "special measures," try the following:

Find out more about handling your finances in IDEA 34, *Love your money.*

Try another idea...

- List the stuff you absolutely have to spend money on to get to your workplace and function at your job—so that's fares and oh, all right, you can have a daily newspaper. No money for lunches (take in your own).

- Allow yourself discretionary spending money. Decide on a reasonable amount for the week—you'll know how much you usually spend each week from writing everything down. Try halving that to begin with. Now you know what happens next. Go to the ATM and take out your basic times five, plus your discretionary—that's what you have to spend in a working week. You can spend the discretionary on what you like but when that's gone, it's gone.

- Use the principle of carrying only what you need at all times. Going to the bar? Estimate how many rounds you'll buy and how much they'll cost and yes, take that with you. When it's gone, you go home.

"I am able to buy anything I want [but] more than anything I hate waste. Uselessness. The things you buy represent how you see yourself—how you wish others to see you. You're a smart cookie. Let the world know it."
OPRAH WINFREY

Defining idea...

How did it go? **Q   I felt like a schoolkid taking just a fiver with me to work. Isn't this a bit stingy?**

A   *Well, yes. But when you were a school kid you probably didn't owe half a year's salary. The idea works on the principle that we spend as much money as we've got in our pocket on garbage. No one's saying don't go to the bar, but if you don't have any spare money on you, you're less likely to visit the drive-thru on the way home. However, there is a school of thought that says, "Carry cash with you at all times, feel abundant. Don't feel mean and more money will come to you." Which is great, but the "cash at all times" school also says "Don't use credit cards, work entirely in cash." If you can do that, it might work better for you.*

Q   I've got a lot of debt but I seem to be making payments. But what if interest rates go up and I start having to pay more? When is enough debt too much?

A   *You may be in trouble if: You have four or more credit commitments; you spend more than 25 percent of your pre-tax income on credit cards and personal loans; you spend more than half your pre-tax income on your mortgage and other credit. If you're asking this question, I think you're worried, and that means stress. So even if you're managing, seek advice. Credit unions are often friendlier and more flexible in their lending.*

38

Take a vacation at your desk

Imbue the old 9-to-5 with a certain glamour and you'll be amazed at how much tension seeps out of your life.

You'll be raising your standards and that means lowering your stress levels.

Forty years has taught me that there are two ways to have a perfect day. One is in the grand tradition of the Lou Reed song. You hang out for a whole day with someone you really, really love who is loving you right back—or at least tolerating you. You don't have to do anything because just being with the beloved is so blissful it blocks out the boring little problems that usually stress you out. If you manage twenty days like this in your whole lifetime, you're doing pretty well.

And then there's the second way. You build a perfect day for yourself and by adding grace and glamour to your life, you remove stress. It takes a little thought. But it is more reliable than true love. You can have a vacation of the mind on even the most mundane day.

REBOOT YOUR COMMUTE

Give your journey to work an overhaul. Set yourself targets. Instead of a drag, see it as a purposeful part of your day. If it involves walking, buy a pedometer. Learn a language. Use the time to repeat your mantras for the day. Be creative: Write a page

Here's an idea for you...

Clothes can play a huge part in improving the quality of our life. Every morning choose one thing that makes your heart sing—a color you love, a fabric that embraces you, a piece of jewelry with sentimental attachment. Next time you're shopping buy clothes that help you radiate confidence.

of freehand prose on the commute in (not if you drive, of course!). Start working up the characters for your novel. It's a terrific time to practice mindfulness, which can deliver the benefits of meditation. The list is endless.

BOOST YOUR ENVIRONMENT

Your starter question: What five changes would make your work environment more pleasant? Here's mine. Getting rid of piles of papers and magazines that need to be filed. Investing in a coffee mug and no more sharing the office's grubby, chipped ones. Cheering up my desk with a bunch of pink tulips. Cleaning my keyboard—so filthy it's a health hazard. Turning down the ringtone volume on my phone. Every day find some way to make your surroundings more pleasant.

BEAT THE MID-AFTERNOON SLUMP

When you feel the slump kicking in, stop working and get away from your workstation if you can. Go for a short walk in the sunshine or take a nap. If you can't, try this: Palm your eyes in your hand for a few minutes and visualize a calm and beautiful place. See this in as much detail as possible.

THE JOURNEY HOME

If your job's the problem, IDEA 40, *How to love the job you've got*, should help.

Try another idea...

This needs a different mood from the journey to work. If you listen to music, make it different from the tunes you play in the morning—slower, deeper. Small stuff like that really helps to emphasize that this is your transition period. Have a project that you work on at this time (planning your vacation is good). And if you read, keep the tone light. If in the morning you read French verbs or the novels of Dostoyevsky, read P. G. Wodehouse on the way home.

SPREAD LOVE

When you pass someone in distress send them "serenity" or "calm" as a thought. Spread good and happy thoughts wherever you go. Smile. Be gracious. Be kind, compassionate, a force for good.

Not every day can be a high day or vacation, but changing your mind-set, looking for grace and sheer fun in previous black holes of misery, turns you into a force for light and transforms your day-to-day grind. It's the art of living lightly and it gets easier the more you look for opportunities to practice your skill.

"You can make more friends in two months by becoming interested in other people than you can in two years by trying to get other people interested in you."
DALE CARNEGIE, founding father of the self-help movement

Defining idea...

How did it go?

Q   This may work for some people but my environment is so depressing, it gets me down. How can I get a lift?

A   *Try this: Repeat to yourself, "Beauty before me. Beauty behind me. Beauty above me. Beauty below me." With each direction look very hard for what is beautiful before you, behind, you, etc. Search for a source of gratification. Do this anywhere, anytime—stuck in traffic, loading the dishwasher, waiting for the bus—and you will be quite amazed at how often you find a source of beauty and wonder in your vicinity. Usually you'll find four. This game also takes some concentration and lifts the spirits, I find. It helps you get out of your normal way of thinking, which makes you more creative.*

Q   I have tried your ideas but still feel stressed at work and feel terrible by mid-afternoon. Am I missing something?

A   *One workplace in eight is as dry as the Sahara. Yes, rehydration is important but turn getting your liter and a half of water into an event. Keep ice on hand, or a twist of lemon. Sip your drinks from a straw. Or choose a different fruit juice every week and have a glass of juice cut with fizzy water. Sure it's fluff. That's the point. Make the everyday special. You could also try my father-in-law's tip that put an end to his mid-afternoon headaches. Stop. Slowly peel an orange. Relish it. (I'd add: Use a napkin and a plate—a sticky keyboard won't help your stress levels!) Really taste that orange. As a general rule, if you do eat at your desk, make as big a deal as you can of it.*

39

You're not paranoid...they *are* out to get you

Are you ready for a journey to the weirder, wilder side?

Relax. We're only talking a little white witchery.

I am just beginning to come out of a period of relatively high stress. In the last few month, my working life has been a strain (some of this is because of office politics) and I've been taken to court by someone whose way of reconciling his conscience to the fact that he's been ripping me off for years is to convince himself that, in fact, it's me who owes him money. Wonderful.

Here is the action plan that I drew up three months ago when this period started: (1) I called my lawyer and got him to deal with all the legal correspondence. Sometimes you need someone on your side. Assuming they're competent, there is absolutely nothing wrong with paying for it. (2) I was scrupulously polite at work, worked extremely diligently, and took pride in what I did while formulating a plan B. (3) I began exercising again—necessary to ground me. (4) I dug out a Tibetan prayer ball that I keep for just such occasions, and I didn't leave the house without it for three months. A Tibetan prayer ball is a pretty little bell that tinkles as you walk and it's believed to protect you against evil spirits.

Here's an idea for you... **When you're feeling stressed and under attack, mechanical repetitive tasks are good for centering you. Cooking works well; so does weeding the garden. Concentrate fully on your actions. Switch off your brain.**

You did what? I can almost hear the thuds as you throw this across the room but hold your fire. In terms of making me feel better, I think number 4 might have been the most useful of all the steps.

Here's the truth: Sometimes the bastards *are* out to get you. I know all the arguments about wishing well to the world, good karma, turning the other cheek. I practice all of them. But sometimes through no fault of your own you become the scapegoat, the victim in life.

Human beings have a very powerful need for scapegoats. No one gets through life without feeling they're being picked on at some time. Money doesn't protect you from it, power doesn't protect you from it. (Some of the most paranoid people in our society have huge reserves of personal wealth and power.) It's incredibly hard to accept that despite your competence and general sweetness of personality, other people don't wish you well. Just remember other people have their own agendas and you don't always know what they are. Sometimes you're blameless and you get the world's opprobrium anyway. So what do you do?

Defining idea... **"I am a kind of paranoiac in reverse. I suspect people of plotting to make me happy."**
J. D. SALINGER

You build up a psychic defense.

"One of the major reasons we feel attacked," writes Caitlin Matthews in the *Psychic Protection Handbook*, "is that we become neglectful of our boundaries, careless with our energy, not noticing when someone or something is taking advantage of us." (Which, incidentally, is exactly why I ended up in court.) Reflect on where your boundaries are weak and sort it out.

Another good way of grounding yourself is by exercising. Bring your mind back to your body as often as you can remember and note what you are feeling. If you're tired, sleep. Eat and drink warm and comforting food. Be in nature. Go to bed with the sunset and rise with the dawn as much as is humanly possible (I realize my Alaskan readers may have a problem doing this). There is great comfort in looking after the basics.

Try the breathing exercise described in IDEA 44, _Out of your head_. Breathing is a great way of building psychic strength.

Try another idea...

One of the simplest methods of boosting your ability to deal with bad karma is to build a shield around you. Sit quietly and find your still center and then imagine a bubble of gold, silver, or rosy pink enclosing your body and your energy field that surrounds your body—otherwise known as your "aura" which you are more likely to be conscious of as your "personal space." Throughout the day remind yourself it's there and see the outside of this shield sparkling and fizzing with energy. On days when I face particular difficulties or stresses, I follow Caitlin Matthews's recommendation and cover myself in imaginary psychic armor. (Practice this before you need it so it comes easily to you.) Breathe out your fear, breathe in courage. Sense a silvery metallic light filling your hands—this is liquid armor. Raise it over your head and smooth it over your body to encase your energy field. If you need more, scoop some up from a pool at your feet in one graceful motion and continue until you feel every part of you is covered in a completely flexible spiritual armor that will mirror back bad vibes. Say aloud, "I am protected. No harm will I give, no harm will I receive." At night mentally peel off your armor. Remember to be grateful for the protection.

"Psychic protection is an ordinary skill for everyday life."
CAITLIN MATTHEWS, author of _The Psychic Protection Handbook_

Defining idea...

How did it go?

Q **I feel under attack and I was with you right up to the part about the psychic armor. This is just nuts, isn't it?**

A *It's not nuts. It's creative visualization. I believe if you try it, you might feel stronger. But perhaps this is a little too New Age for you and you'd feel happier with a traditional prayer. Try this one, known as "St. Patrick's Breastplate": "Christ with me, Christ before me, Christ behind me, Christ in me, Christ beneath me, Christ above me, Christ on my right, Christ on my left, Christ when I lie down, Christ when I sit down, Christ in the heart of every man who thinks of me, Christ in the mouth of every man who speaks of me." You are saying exactly the same thing—arm me, protect me, let no one harm me. Again, remember to say thank you for the protection.*

Q **So where do I get a Tibetan prayer ball?**

A *In any New Age shop. These prayer balls are round and silver and have a pleasing ring. You could also carry one of the more ubiquitous talismans, like a St. Christopher. Or you could make your own. Carry any symbol or token that you have dedicated to protecting you. But don't get too hung up on it. Talismans are there to remind you to pay attention and be careful. They don't do the work. You do that.*

40

How to love the job you've got

Sometimes you can't have the one you want. So you have to love the one you've got.

One in four of us wants to leave our jobs. We can't all do it at once, so here's how to cope until your personal Great Escape.

THE BOTTOM LINE

Hate your job? It's probably for three reasons—you hate the work (it's monotonous or stressful); you hate the environment, including your colleagues; something else has happened in your life that makes work seem meaningless and you're ready for a lifestyle change. Or it could be that you're in denial. I'm going to seem a bit mystical here, because I firmly believe that sometimes we hate our job because we can't be bothered to address what's really stressing us out in our lives. Our energy is focused elsewhere and until we figure out whatever drama or sadness is soaking up our concentration, we're not likely to find our dream job any time soon. So the advice here is not about refocusing your résumé—there are plenty of other places where you can read up on that. But it will help you relieve stress in the short

Here's an idea for you... **Boost work morale in a stressful workplace by starting group traditions beyond getting drunk on Friday night and moaning. Go out for Chinese on payday or book a day at a spa or celebrate every birthday with champagne and cake.**

term and make you feel better about yourself in the long term. And that, hopefully, will help you raise your energy enough to eventually find another job.

LOVE YOUR SURROUNDINGS...

...Just as much as you can. If your workplace is grim and dreary, you are not going to feel good. Clear your desk. Sort out clutter. Personalize your work space with objects of beauty and grace. Pin up photos of beautiful vistas you've visited or would like to visit. (It's a bit less personal than family pictures.) But whatever you choose to put on your desk, change the visuals every couple of weeks; otherwise your brain stops registering them.

LOVE YOUR LUNCH BREAKS

A lunch break shouldn't be a scramble for bad food and a desultory walk around a shopping mall. Spend time planning. Every lunch hour should involve movement, fresh air, delicious healthy food, and at least one work of art. Works of art are easily available for your perusal (art galleries, department stores) and easily transportable (books, CDs). Always, always take an hour to relax at lunch.

LOVE YOUR COLLEAGUES

Tough one. These could well be the reason you hate your job in the first place. If there are people who specifically annoy you, then find a way to deal with them.

Your local bookstore is full of manuals that will teach you how. Allow yourself no more than 5 minutes a day unloading your woes about work colleagues to a trusted friend or partner—not

Check out IDEA 50, *Burned out?*, for more on surviving extreme stress.

Try another idea...

anyone you work with. This is not goody-goody—it's self-preservation. The more you unload your negativity all over the place, the more you are talking yourself into a hole of unhappiness and stress.

LOVE YOURSELF

Show up. Work hard. Do better. Lots of people who are unhappy with their work kid themselves that they are working really hard, when in fact their work is shoddy and second-rate. If you're not up to speed, improve your knowledge base and skills. If your work is lazy, look at everything you produce or every service you offer and ask yourself how you can make it special, imbue it with your uniqueness, breathe creativity and a little bit of love into it. Doing every task diligently and with positivity will vastly increase your self-esteem.

LOVE YOUR DREAMS

Most of us couldn't have gotten through school without the ability to drift away on a pleasant reverie of future plans. For 5 minutes in every hour allow yourself to dream. Read through job pages that aren't related to your present job. You may see a position or course that fires your imagination in a completely new direction.

"People get disturbed not so much by events but by the view which they take of them."
EPICTETUS

Defining idea...

How did it go?

Q I'm following your advice, so how come I'm still sad?

A *Improve the quality of your life outside work. Build a social life you can look forward to, full of variety, stimulation, and zing. Create a home you can't wait to get back to that truly nourishes and nurtures you. Learn something new, stretch your mind and imagination. And get out and meet people. The people you know are a very valuable resource. They inspire you. They introduce you to other people. They give you ideas. Don't specifically network but always be open to meeting new people and be the first one to chat to a new person introduced to your group. Find out what makes them tick. People who are open and kind to other people, respectful of others' ideas and competence, and interested in their lives, are exactly the sort of people who end up living their dream lives with their dream jobs. Don't tell me it's coincidence.*

Q I do have dreams, but I won't be able to earn enough money if I follow them. How can I get over this hurdle?

A *Write down all your fears about changing careers and then start writing ways you could save money or earn more. Energetic, focused people have opportunities thrown at them and I've never met one who I thought of as being broke. Speed up the process somewhat by repeating out loud several times a day, "Wonderful opportunities and plenty of money are the rightful rewards for all my talent and brightness and hard work."*

41

Stop acting on impulse

Focus, concentration, sticking to what you've started. That will cut your stress levels instantly.

Yes, yes, yes. But how?

Some days I run around like a frantic hen. Charging to work, rushing home early to spend time with the kids, doing chores, doing research, calling my mother. I react to events and whatever crisis looms next. I don't do anything correctly. I don't do some things at all.

When I get to bed I remember the stuff that I didn't get around to and feel disappointed and frustrated with myself. When that happens it's time to go back to basics and use this idea. It helps you finish what you start and makes you feel on top of your life. Besides helping you become more focused, it also helps you curb your impulse to wander off and do other stuff rather than the one task that you have set yourself. It will show up the numerous times you have just gotten started on a project when it suddenly seems terribly important to water the plants, call your mother, or make a nice cup of tea. But now you will be prepared and will observe your impulses as just that—impulses. And you will stay put with a wise "Oh, there I go, looking for ways to waste time again."

Besides training you to focus and resist the impulse to waste time, this idea will achieve two further objectives: (1) It will build your self-esteem by fostering your sense of yourself as a person who follows through on their word. (2) It will clear

Here's an idea for you...

Making a promise to yourself every night and keeping it the next day is the route to mental toughness. Every time you keep a promise to yourself, stick some loose change in a jar. It's a good visual record of your growing focus and strength— and, of course, you get to spend the cash at the end of it.

your life of a ton of annoying little irritations that have been stopping you mentally from moving on.

Step 1. Before you go to bed tonight, think of something you want to achieve tomorrow. Keep it really small and simple. It doesn't matter what it is, but you have to do it. Make it something restful—you're going to read a chapter of a favorite novel. Make it useful— you're going to clean the cutlery drawer. Make it worthy—you're going to take a multivitamin. Take this promise extremely seriously. Promise yourself you'll do it and follow through. If you don't, no excuses. You've failed, but maybe you're aiming too high. Make your next promise easier to achieve.

Step 2. Make a promise to yourself every evening for a week. And follow through.

Step 3. OK, now you're going to make a list of some tasks that you need to undertake but have been putting off. You will need seven, one for every day of the week. Some ideas: Starting on your tax return; making a dental appointment; canceling the gym membership you never use; cleaning out your closet; cleaning out the inside of the car; tackling just one pile from the many piles on your desk; grooming the dog; getting a start on cleaning the garage.

Step 4. Write these down and keep them by your bed. Each night for the next week, pick one and promise yourself you'll do it tomorrow.

This is a great one to use in relation to IDEA 30, *Zap those piles*.

Try another idea...

Step 5. Write another list. This time put on it things that are worrying you and driving you crazy. Suggestions: Discover if your retirement plan will pay out enough for you to live on; write a letter to that friend you're upset with; paint the kitchen. Put on the list everything that is driving you nuts. Then pick one and break it down into manageable steps. Promise yourself to do the first of these steps tomorrow, and every day from now on, make a promise to take another step forward. Don't let impulse drive you off course.

This is an exercise in mental toughness. Making promises to yourself that you never keep brings you down and, over time, breaks your heart. But by breaking difficult tasks down into manageable chunks and building the strength of character to follow through and get them out of the way, you take a huge step forward in reducing stress in your life.

Warning: Don't make more than two or three promises a day. Keep it simple.

"He who every morning plans the transactions of the day and follows out that plan, carries a thread that will guide him through the maze of the most busy life. But where no plan is laid, where the disposal of time is surrendered merely to the chance of incidence, chaos will soon reign."
VICTOR HUGO

Defining idea...

How did
it go?

Q **I'm focusing the best I can, but I'm sticking to pleasurable things so it's easy. Am I cheating?**

A *No, stick with it. Prioritizing pleasure is really good for you anyway. And the important thing is that you're learning mental discipline. Then you'll be ready to overcome what's known in coaching circles as your "tolerations." Whether it's an untidy home, broken appliances, a bad filing system— everything that gets on your nerves, brings you down, and saps your energy—and stops you from reaching your potential. But the really pernicious thing about tolerations is that after a while, we cease to notice them. They drop off our radar but they're still there, bitching up our lives. So start with pleasure, move on to tolerations, and then you'll be ready for the really big stuff—dealing with your mother-in-law, your boss, and the fact that you hate your job. And it all starts by keeping just one promise to yourself a day.*

Q **How does sticking to a task boost my self-esteem?**

A *Because we usually achieve a ton of stuff but are so busy beating ourselves up for what we didn't do that we don't notice. This way you get more conscious of what you do achieve and you take the time to go, "Look, I got that done. Aren't I fabulous?" You are building yourself up for success, not failure.*

42

Take the stress out of your love life

Too stressed to talk? Remember, divorce is pretty stressful, too.

Stress-proof your relationship and everything else will fall into place—eventually.

There is absolutely no point in reading on until you put this idea to improve your relationship into action: It is the sine qua non of relationships. Once a week minimum, you and your partner have a "date," where you focus completely on each other and nothing else. It may only be for a few hours. It doesn't have to involve a lot of money. You don't even have to go out—although I strongly recommend it. (Couples who spend too much time hanging around the same small space tend to lose that loving feeling.) Seeing your love in a new environment helps keep love alive, even if it's only in your local park. But whatever you do, you must spend at least a couple of hours a week talking to each other or you are taking a mighty big gamble with your love.

Here's an idea for you... **Get into bed. Whichever one is feeling emotionally stronger should spoon around the other. Hold your hands entwined resting on the recipient's heart. Regularize your breathing so you exhale and inhale at the same time. Lie there and breathe in unison.**

If you want something, ask for it

Second-guessing what your partner thinks or feels is such a waste of time. You're nearly always wrong, and your assumptions lead to fights. You might assume your partner can see that you spending five hours a night on housework is unfair. On the other hand you might assume your partner can see that sex once a month isn't going to win you any prizes in a "red-hot couple of the year" competition. (The two may well be related, by the way.) However, you could be assuming wrong. Do the work yourself first. Figure out what you want to make you happy. Then let your partner know. It might end up as a compromise, but you've at least got a chance of getting it this way.

Keep surprising each other

No, not with the news of your affair with Geoff in accounting. To re-create the passion of your first romance, you have to see each other through new eyes. To do that you have to be passionate, engaged in your life, interested in the world. If you're not fascinated by your life, you can hardly expect anyone else to be. And remember the power of spontaneity. Plan to be spontaneous. Take turns surprising each other, even if it's only with takeout—although the occasional weekend away would be better.

Constantly plan and dream

A relationship that doesn't move forward will die. You have to dream big. Whether it's planning your next vacation, your fantasy house, another child, a move to the country. Not all these plans have to come to fruition, but you have to build common dreams and turn some of them into goals that you're working toward as a team.

Have sex

Call me old-fashioned, but I think this is important. Lots of couples don't, of course, but I would say that unless you're both absolutely happy with this (are you sure? See first item on this list), then you're sitting on a potentially huge stressor.

Give your lover what they need to feel loved

This can melt away stress in a relationship. Find out what your partner needs to feel loved—meals out, compliments, sex, praise in front of your friends, chocolates on demand. Ask. Then give it. Often. There is absolutely no use in you saying you love your partner, or showing them that you love them *in your way*, if they don't feel loved at the end of it. When your home life is stressed, ask your partner "Do you feel loved?" And if the answer's no, do something about it.

Read more about the power of connection in IDEA 48, *Reach out*.

Try another idea...

"My wife and I were happy for twenty years. Then we met."
RODNEY DANGERFIELD, comedian

Defining idea...

How did it go?

Q **We've set time aside to talk but we can't stop arguing. Is this fighting useful?**

A *Nothing wrong with arguing, as long as it has a point. Where is this going? What do you want? What does your partner want? Can you ever reach a compromise? If you're just mindlessly bellowing at each other, are you letting off steam? Again, that's all right now and again. But if that's your relationship, you need to stop shouting long enough to try some other methods—talking quietly, mediation, counseling. Because if the fights aren't resolving anything and not serving any purpose, it means you have to find new ways of communicating.*

Q **I want sex much more than my wife. Having practically no sex stresses me out. What's the answer?**

A *Even if you can't persuade her every time to have sex, insist on cuddles and physical closeness. Physical closeness without pressure to perform may boost her libido. But even if it doesn't, you are entitled to physical closeness. Without touch, humans get very touchy indeed. They get stressed. So stressed they get ill. I can't emphasize the importance of touch strongly enough. There is a theory that the reason women have clitorises in the first place is to encourage them to have sex, because if they weren't having sex, they wouldn't get touched enough to stay emotionally healthy. That's one for all humans to think about before they say "not tonight."*

43

Perfect moments

The ability to create perfect moments is possibly the most valuable life skill you'll ever learn.

It's the only guarantee that tomorrow will be less stressed than today.

We humans are lousy at predicting what will make us happy. We work our butts off to get the "right" job. We scrimp and save for the big house and flashy car. We think surely parenthood will make us really, really happy—and it does for a few years, until our adorable toddlers grow into worrisome teens. Human happiness is the holy grail, but no one yet has found a formula for it.

Or have they? In the last few years, neuroscientists have moved their attention from what's going wrong in the brains of depressed people to exploring what's going right in the brains of happy people. And for the most part, it's quite simple.

Happy people don't get so busy stressing about building a "perfect" tomorrow that they forget to enjoy this "perfect" today.

It turns out that the surest, indeed, the *only* predictor of how happy you are going to be in the future is how good you are at being happy today. If you want to know if you are going to be stressed out tomorrow, ask yourself what you are doing to diminish your stress today. And if the answer's nothing, don't hold your breath. You

Here's an
idea for
you... **Invest in an old-fashioned
teakettle. Starting off with a
cup of tea in bed can get the day
off to a good beginning with a
little effort on your part.**

won't be that calm and serene person you long
to be any time soon.

We can plan the perfect wedding, perfect
party, perfect marriage, perfect career. But we
have absolutely no idea if when we get there,
a perfect anything is going to be delivered. The only thing we can do is guarantee
that today at least we will have a perfect moment—a moment of no stress where
we pursue pure joy.

What is a perfect moment for you? I can't tell. For me it is whatever helps trigger
me to remember that unknown, unquantifiable, profoundly peaceful part of myself.
Let's call it "the spirit." We could call it "Joe," but that lacks that certain mystical
something that I'm aiming for. Anyway, when I'm having a perfect moment, I'm
absolutely happy, absolutely content. That doesn't mean everything is all right in my
life, but it does mean that for this one moment, I've got enough to feel joyful.

Some people slip in to a perfect moment as easily as putting on an old coat. But me,
I'm a pragmatist. I think if you want to have a perfect moment, you have to plan for
it early, before your day is hijacked. So I try to start each day with a perfect moment.
All debris, mess, and clutter is banished from my bedroom the night before. When I
wake just about the first thing I see is a bunch of fresh-cut flowers—big, squashy
pink peonies are a favorite. Before my eyes are quite open, I reach out and grab a
book of poetry from my side table and I read for five minutes. I choose poetry
because it reminds me that life is a lot bigger than me and infinitely more
interesting.

But your perfect moment might be snatched late at night, listening to jazz by candlelight when the family is asleep. Or it could be a glass of chilled wine as the sun slips beyond the horizon. You might best be able to access a perfect moment by running around your park or through practicing yoga. Listening to music while you exercise often heightens the sensations of being in tune with your body and tips you into joy. Preparing, cooking, and eating food can give perfect moments. Gardening is a good one. Sex is reliable. We all know the sensation of feeling "bigger" than ourselves. All you have to do is give yourself the space to feel it more often—ideally, at least once a day.

Combine this with elements of mindfulness, which you'll find described in IDEA 44, *Out of your head.*

Try another idea...

But ultimately, only you know your own triggers. Write down a week's worth and plan for them. Schedule them in your diary. It obviously doesn't have to be the same activity every day and sometimes despite your best intentions, it all goes belly up. (I only get to read poetry when I'm not woken by the kids clamoring for cartoons and cereal.)

But planning for perfect moments means they are more likely to happen. Even if you don't believe now that striving for perfect moments will de-stress you, try it. At least you will be able to say, "Today, there were five minutes where I stopped and enjoyed life." Enjoying life today is the only certainty you have of happiness and your best chance of being less stressed tomorrow.

"Happiness not in another place, but this place...not for another hour, but this hour."
WALT WHITMAN

Defining idea...

How did it go?

Q   Don't I need more than just moments of stress-free living?

A   Once you start building perfect moments you'll find they show up spontaneously in your life. You'll find yourself stopping to notice the way the sunlight hits your kitchen table. Or buying a bunch of flowers just because they look pretty. Perfect moments soon become perfect half-hours, perfect afternoons, perfect weeks. But I don't want to freak out the stressed-out workaholics. Let's start small.

Q   I've tried, but having a cup of tea when I've got a million things to do just doesn't work. Any more bright ideas?

A   Get outside if at all possible. Nature works on a very deep level to help you feel connected. What you are seeking is to experience being in "the flow" as it was described by famous psychologist Mihaly Csikszentmihaly. Being in the flow means being totally absorbed in whatever it is that we are doing, at peace with ourselves and the world. Being outside helps combat that feeling of being harried and trapped by our demanding world. Breathe. Feel the weather. You're not just seeking beauty—it's a matter of connection with the bigger picture.

44

Out of your head

A way of handling stress that could improve your sex life, too.

If you want to win the battle against stress, pay attention to everything— except what's going on in your head.

Just about everything else you'll read on stress will tell you to meditate to beat it. Good idea. Meditation is incredibly effective. Hundreds of research studies prove that it reduces hypertension, cholesterol, and a load of other markers of stress-induced illness. It gives you more energy, a happier disposition, and a better sex life.

I want to be a meditator. God knows, I've tried. Like senior discounts and elastic-waist pants it's something I'm looking forward to in my later years. In the meantime, I will use an idea that delivers much of the benefits without all the spiritual expectations, and is easy to bring into play whenever you need it. A sort of meditation-lite, if you like.

Mindfulness came out of the work of Jon Kabat-Zinn (author of the fabulously titled *Full Catastrophe Living*), a scientist who runs stress-reduction programs at the University of Massachusetts Medical Center. Kabat-Zinn wanted to find a way of teaching patients how to kick-start their own healing powers. Like meditation, mindfulness gives control by helping you to listen to your body.

Here's an idea for you... **Make your morning shower a mini-meditation session through the power of mindfulness. Listen to the sound of the water and feel the sensation of the water on your skin. Let thoughts float down the drain, concentrate only on what your body can feel, see, and hear.**

Lie down (although you can do this sitting if it is more convenient). It helps at first to close your eyes. Become aware of your breathing. Don't force deep breaths but "see" in your mind your breath entering through your nostrils and flooding your lungs. Listen to the sounds of your breath. Concentrate on nothing else. When your mind wanders, let these thoughts float away, imagine them as little white clouds, and return to the breath.

(That's it.)

It's recommended you be mindful for 45 minutes a day for best results. If you can manage just 5 minutes (which is all I fit in most days), you will find it helps immensely. This keeps you calm when things gets hairy and seems to work especially well for maintaining your sense of humor when life seems dire. It appears to have all sorts of health benefits, too—aiding healing and lowering blood pressure.

It is also not necessarily as easy as it sounds. Stopping and listening and just being allows you to access great joy and happiness, but it also makes it hard to ignore feelings of grief and anger and disappointment that surface when you stop whirling around in a frantic rush long enough to listen to them. If these feelings arise for you, pay attention. Kabat-Zinn says that practicing mindfulness helps his patients learn what they really want from life, and after it becomes second nature to become still and focused, he recommends that you ask yourself questions during your mindfulness sessions such as "What do I truly love?" and "Where am I going?"

Read IDEA 9, *Relaxation—what we can learn from the cavemen.* **Mindfulness works well as a mini-relaxation break.**

Try another idea...

The point of this is to make you more aware of the here and now. It is quite shocking when you realize how often your mind is occupied with running over what has happened in the past and fantasizing about what might happen in the future (and fantasy is all it is. None of us can know what's going to happen). The here and now is a great place to be—because nearly always in the here and now you are absolutely fine. Mindfulness transports you away from fear and toward self-reliance and self-confidence. You can use it when you're brushing your teeth. You can use it when you're having sex. It will automatically make any activity more profound and you more calm.

With practice you will find yourself falling into the mindfulness state at odd times—making dinner, crossing the road, in the middle of a conversation with your bank. This is the best way of turning "space" into "useful experiences."

"Now's the day and now's the hour."
ROBERT BURNS

Defining idea...

How did it go?

Q   I'm still struggling to find five quiet minutes a day. How can I make time for mindfulness?

A   *The marvelous thing about mindfulness is that you can use it whenever you remember to and you'll find it intensifies sensations and helps you relax. When you're having sex, become aware of the moment; touch, smell, sensation, sight. Switch off your mind and concentrate fully on what you are doing right now. It de-stresses you and improves your sex life, too. Similarly, when you are walking, use the steps along with the breath to focus on the moment. Notice the breeze on your cheek, the birdsong, the scent of the flowers. Concentrate on right here, right now and the world slows right down.*

Q   I just can't concentrate. My mind runs away with me. How do I learn to focus?

A   *Concentrate intensely on your breath. I find these breathing patterns recommended by author Caitlin Matthews work well because concentrating on the breaths helps still my mind. The Well-being Breath helps get control of panic: Inhale 8; hold in 8; exhale 8; hold out 4. The Creative Breath helps you become more creative and intuitive: Inhale 4; hold in 8; exhale 16; hold out 4. The Sleep Breath helps soothe you to sleep: Inhale 4; hold in 8; exhale 32; hold out 4.*

45

Aromatherapy master class

Think that aromatherapy is just for wimps? Wrong. Aromatherapy has attitude. Aromatherapy kicks butt. Aromatherapy actually works.

Here's a challenge. Next time you're writing your to-do list, put "Do something nice for me" at the top of the list and give it top priority.

If you're laughing at the very thought of such self-indulgence, then you need this idea because it works fast. Aromatherapy is a bit of a joke. How often have you read "Sprinkle a little lavender oil in your bath to de-stress you"? How often have you wondered how you'll find the time for a shower, much less a bath?

Let's face it, the people who can find the time to do the lavender oil stuff probably don't have too much stress in the first place. And I thought so, too, until I interviewed Judith White, an inspirational aromatherapist who believes aromatherapy can do a lot more than make your bath smell nice. "Aromatherapy is perfect for those times when you have only seconds because it works in seconds

Here's an idea for you...

For days when you have to think fast, carry around a hankie with some peppermint oil sprinkled on it and sniff it to help you get focus. Studies have shown it aids concentration.

and it is one of the most valuable tools we have to help us live a less stressed, happier life," she says. She speaks from personal experience. "I had to learn how to keep myself on an equilibrium when my previous business left me emotionally, mentally, and physically stressed for an extremely difficult few years. My oils were my greatest ally. That, and taking responsibility for the situation I was in."

Judith is very into the idea that it is empowering for us all, but especially women, to accept that they are not victims, that they helped create problems in their lives and it's up to them to change their situation for the better. "When we take responsibility for our lives we automatically start looking after ourselves. We realize that it isn't selfish to put ourselves first now and then because we are taking responsibility for the effect our 'victim' mode has on others. Think about the impact a woman's energy has within her home on her partner and kids. If a woman has a good day and her partner a bad one, he will soon be uplifted if she maintains her good spirits. On the other hand, if a man has a great day, but the woman is down, then you will quickly watch his great day evaporate as her energy dominates. Women have the energetic ability to sweep away everyone else's enthusiasm along with their own. Women's power over others is

Defining idea...

"Smell is a potent wizard that transports you across thousands of miles and all the years you have lived."
HELEN KELLER

immense because we are the great intuitives and communicators and we can use these skills positively or negatively to affect others."

She recommends you look for opportunities throughout your day to stick in a mini-multitasking treatment. Here are some I've found helpful. Oils aren't just for baths. When showering, cover the drain with a washcloth and add 4–6 drops (in total) of a combination of essential oils to the shower. Add one drop of essential oil to your existing moisturizer. Inhale deeply as you apply it. Try soaking your feet in an aromatic footbath while reading or watching TV. For an immediate treatment put a couple of drops of essential oil into the middle of a hot, wet washcloth, wring it out, hold it over your face, and breathe deeply.

For more on taking responsibility see IDEA 15, *A shortcut to coping with obstacles.*

Try another idea...

"Always remember essential oils are highly volatile, very powerful natural essences. Working with them is like working with magic. And what is magic? Magic is energy."
JANINE MURPHY, writing in *Aromatherapy Today*

Defining idea...

How did
it go?

Q **I'm skeptical that these can work. Where's the scientific evidence?**

A *Research into aromatherapy is still ongoing. One way it's been shown to work is by the molecules of oil being picked up via the mucous membranes of the nose and from there affecting the limbic system of the brain. This is one of the more "ancient" parts of the human brain, connected to memory and instinct. Which is why it might have such a profound effect on mood. I do understand your doubts but by using it quite aggressively—reaching for an oil at any moment of stress—as a method of calming me down fast, I have found it useful. By building up an "armory" of oils, I have become more of a devotee over the years. And it's worth remembering that doctors caution pregnant women not to use certain oils without checking with them first—which they'd hardly bother to do if there weren't therapeutic as well as fragrant issues at stake.*

Q **So what oils should I use and in what quantities?**

A *Add 10-20 drops to a bath, 3-5 to a burner. Lavender is great when you need to calm down or drift off to sleep. Cedarwood is good when you're anxious or stressed. Geranium is good for making you feel in control. Grapefruit or may chang for when you're feeling down. Clary sage when you're feeling paranoid or oversensitive (but avoid this when you're pregnant, which is a shame, because that's just when you might be likely to need it), and ylang ylang when you want to boost your self-esteem and feel confident and sensual.*

46

Tame your to-do list

The problem with to-do lists is that it takes seconds to scribble yet another entry—and a whole lot longer to get around to doing it.

The essential thing to remember is that you actually need to schedule the time to do your to-do list or else it's just another source of stress.

What revolutionized the to-do list for me was the idea of work days, buffer days, and free days. In my experience, everything you ever need to do falls into one of these three categories. *Work days*—self-explanatory. *Free days*—fun days, and these should be a complete break from work. These are for rest and recreation, and if you don't think there is time for this, remember recreation is just that—the time to re-create, and what you're re-creating is yourself. If you don't have at least one of these a week you're going to end up stressed out and useless. *Buffer days*—these are so-called because they act as a buffer against stress. These are the days you get on top of all those little things that need to get done—filing receipts, updating your résumé. These are never as important as other things—until your tax return is due tomorrow or you lose your job. Buffer days are those times when you truly stress-proof your life in advance.

Here's an idea for you...

When you complete an item on your to-do list, instead of putting a line through it, mark it through with a colorful highlighter pen. This raises your spirits and makes you feel you've achieved more. The more color on the page, the more you've gotten through.

Step 1. Prepare the master list. You need a notebook in which you write down everything that needs doing, now or in the future, important or unimportant. I know a fashion editor who has her special book of lists, a beautiful leather one in which she writes lists for everything—presents, places she wants to visit, books she wants to read—as well as all the humdrum stuff. I like her book. It turns the to-do list into a creative act. If the idea appeals to you, I urge you to purchase one.

Step 2. OK, now that you have your list, divide it into two. You can do this with two different colored marker pens. One half will be stuff you have to do (insuring the car, buying your son a birthday present, finishing a work project), the other half will be the wish list, stuff you'd like to do in an ideal world (sorting out your photos, clearing out the cupboard you haven't looked into since 1987).

Step 3. Now get your calendar. You can use your planner, but a calendar works better. I like a big one with a month on a page. Mark out work days, buffer days, and free days. Decide on the top five things on your "must-do" list—some of these will be work, some will be buffer. Schedule these in on your calendar at the next appropriate session. I recommend color coding. You could use three different colors of pen for the different kinds of days, but I use three different colored mini Post-it Notes—work, buffer, and free—putting a task down on a separate Post-it Note and sticking it on the appropriate day. The reason for the multicolored stuff is that you can see at a glance when your life is getting out of balance. It gives you an immediate visual reference of where you're spending your time.

This can be applied to any big task, such as organizing your home—see IDEA 30, *Zap those piles.*

Try another idea...

Step 4. Look at your wish list. Pick three things on it. These will probably fall into buffer or free days. If you look forward to it with unalloyed pleasure, it's for a free day. If there is any element of duty whatsoever, it's a buffer. Scribble these on appropriate color-coded Post-it Notes and stick them on the calendar. Every evening rip off the Post-it Notes for the next day and transfer them to your planner, toss 'em in the trash when you've completed them (which is very satisfying). And if you don't get something completed, take it home and find another slot for it on your calendar. If you don't use Post-it Notes, just scribble the items for the next day in your planner each evening or transfer them to your PDA.

What have you achieved besides a multicolored calendar bristling with Post-it Notes? A lot. You have prioritized your time and you've allocated all the urgent things a time slot. You've also prioritized some of the non-urgent ones, thus achieving the mythical life–work balance.

"My happiness is not the means to any end. It is the end."
AYN RAND, author

Defining idea...

How did
it go?

Q **It all sounds a little kindergarten-ish. Can it really help?**

A *It does. That's why it's good fun. It was taught to me by a life coach and it works really well if, like me, you like stationery. But the basic principle is that you allocate a time slot for every task you want to achieve. That's all you've got to take from this idea, but the color coding is especially useful if you're self-employed. It not only reminds you that you haven't had a day off for a week, but it also shows you when you are spending too much valuable time administrating (buffering—useful but not actively bringing in money) rather than drumming up business (working).*

Q **I just can't justify spending a whole day on buffer activities. What can I do?**

A *Fair enough. Go for a buffer morning, afternoon, or evening. But in practice, I find you don't get much done if you don't manage at least three hours of concentrated buffering.*

47

Cherish yourself

Surveys show that we know exactly what we ought to do in order to relax. We just can't be bothered.

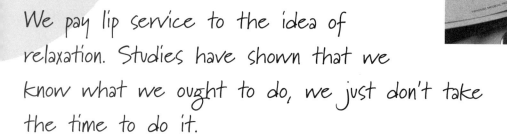

We pay lip service to the idea of relaxation. Studies have shown that we know what we ought to do, we just don't take the time to do it.

The solution is to build rock-solid relaxation time into your schedule and treat your appointment to relax as seriously as you do any other. If at all possible, book a professional relaxation therapy session once a week. Failing that, schedule time once a month for a DIY treatment at home.

In a professional capacity I've tried every kind of therapy available and below are my two favorites for relaxation. This is not purely subjective. For the sake of research (and because a newspaper was paying me), I had every kind of de-stressing therapy administered while hooked up to a heart rate monitor. Flotation and reflexology lowered my heart rate the most.

Here's an idea for you...

Try a quick stretch for instant relaxation. Sit facing a wall. Place your feet on the wall and bring your legs up so that the wall supports them. Edge closer so your backside is only inches from the wall. Lie still and breathe. Support the base of your spine with a cushion if necessary.

FLOTATION

Floating naked in pitch darkness and utter silence for an hour at a time in heavily salted water isn't everyone's cup of tea. (Hint: Don't shave before you go—flotation is hell on nicks.) Some flotation tanks now allow you to listen to music or have a small light burning throughout but I urge you to at least try the hardcore version unless you are claustrophobic. Sensory deprivation is the closest you can get to experiencing the security and comfort of the womb. You are all alone with your thoughts—and, personally, the utter banality of my thoughts came as a shock. But after a while you become disoriented and that's when the magic happens. I know people who have had almost mystical experiences. Others have had the brightest ideas of their lives while floating. Personally, I've never had such an epiphany but I have felt relaxed and energized for days afterward. A monthly or, even better, weekly float can really help. This for me is the big daddy of relaxation techniques.

DIY version

Run a bath as deep as you dare. Empty one packet of Dead Sea Salts or Epsom salts (at least 500 grams) into your bath. Make the bathroom as dark as possible. Set an alarm clock for half an hour. Soak in the bath and sip herbal tea or water throughout to prevent dehydration. (Hot drinks increase perspiration, which is good.) Don't do this if you are pregnant, have high blood pressure, diabetes, or any kind of heart problem. Don't dry off after your bath, but wrap yourself in towels and go straight to bed. Be careful. You may feel light-headed. When you wake, take a warm bath or shower.

REFLEXOLOGY

Ancient Egyptian tomb paintings depict scenes of pharaohs getting their feet fiddled with.

Reflexology is an old, old treatment. It is far more sophisticated than a mere foot rub, though that's not to be sneezed at. Having your feet cradled and massaged grounds you and is instantly calming. The theory is that all nerves originate in the spine and branch out through the body, but ultimately all connect with the nerves that end in the foot. Each area of the foot therefore corresponds to an area of the body.

DIY version

First, relax your feet in a foot bath into which you've added some tepid water and a few drops of peppermint oil. Then gently massage your feet using your thumb to make small circling movements over the whole sole of each foot. When you find a tender spot, work on it gently—this indicates an area where you have tension. Personally, I find rubbing the foot just below the little toe, just under the joint, relaxing. Apparently it corresponds to the shoulders. Another place I've found it worth pressing (although I'm not sure it's strictly reflexology) is the furrow on the top of your foot where the bones of your first and second toes meet.

For more on DIY relaxation, check out IDEA 45, *Aromatherapy master class.*

Try another idea...

"There is no need to go to India or anywhere else to find peace. You will find that deep place of silence right in your room, your garden, or even your bathtub."
ELISABETH KÜBLER-ROSS, psychiatrist

Defining idea...

How did it go?

Q Isn't a massage a fine way to relax?

A *Of course, massage is a great de-stressing tool. But a lot can depend on the quality of the therapist. A bad massage in disruptive surroundings actually raises my stress levels ("Why am I paying $60 for this?") so I'd urge you to keep searching until you find someone good. Ideally, close to where you live because nothing beats falling right into bed after a good massage. I'd also recommend a particular form of massage: hot stone therapy, which involves the application of hot and cold stones. It sounds horrendous but it appears to work on a deep level to remove tension in the muscles.*

Q I'm thinking of yoga. Does it work for stress?

A *Absolutely. Studies have shown that yoga lowers blood pressure and relaxes you deeply after just 25 minutes. There is no question that classes work best of all. But if you can't get to them regularly, at least master the sun salute. This is a series of movements (best carried out in the morning, facing the sun, ideally) that work together to support your adrenal glands. You can learn it in minutes from a good yoga book or teacher. It gets the day off to a great start and anchors you—doing it every morning gives us some continuity in our chaotic lives.*

48

Reach out

Touchy-feely behavior is the best stress buster of all. Time to give love and, hopefully, get some back.

And if you're not getting it from the people around you, time to ditch them and find some people who are willing to play along.

In general, women are better at dealing with stress than men. It's one explanation given for the fact that they tend to live longer. Science has proven it. It discovered that although both males and females experienced the "fight or flight" response, women had another way of dealing with stress—the "tend and befriend" response. When women perceived danger their almost instantaneous reaction is to look after those weaker than themselves (classically, their children) and to reach out to others for comfort and support. This resulted in the release of the hormone oxytocin, which is powerfully de-stressing. So what can we learn from this?

Men suck.   (Sorry, sorry. No, they don't. Just couldn't resist it.)

Seriously, now. What we can learn from tend and befriend is it's important to…

Here's an idea for you...

When you're in the middle of an argument with a loved one, try this. Think about life from their point of view. What stresses are they under right now? Why do you think they are behaving in this particularly annoying way? Imagine love pouring from your heart to surround them in an imaginary hug. It's very hard to stay angry with someone when you begin to think gently of them and it can defuse stressful, blood-pressure-raising anger almost immediately.

Make friends.   People with friends of all ages—younger *and* older than themselves—tend to look younger and feel younger than those who restrict themselves to their own age group, and to be less stressed. Social isolation is linked with poor survival rates in patients with coronary artery disease. Patients with three or fewer people in their social network were more than twice as likely to die as those with more people around them.

We need *friends*—not just acquaintances. As we get older, we tend simply not to have the time to keep up with the friends we've got already, much less make new ones. But it might be time to radically alter your attitude toward friendship. Look long and hard at your friendships: Are they satisfying emotionally or have they been stale and just a bit boring for years? If you do not have a group of people who love, cherish, and delight you, then seek them out. This might very well mean seeing less of friends that you've already got. This sounds harsh but feeling that we have soul mates is a very important part of staying stress-free. In every work and social situation, look for the people that interest you, not the ones that you think would be interested in you. Reach out to them, try to befriend them. Don't let small details like their age or clothes put you off. We tend to get rigid ideas of what our social peer group is but we can always break out of it. There's barely a person alive who won't be flattered by your interest, so if you like the look of a person—if they look interesting and engaged in the world—approach and make friends.

If your relationship needs a boost, take a look at IDEA 42, Take the stress out of your love life.

Try another idea...

Volunteer.   Doing something positive for your community is a fantastic way of looking after yourself. A survey of volunteers discovered that around 63 percent reported that giving up their time to help others lowered their stress levels. (It also combated feelings of depression in around 50 percent.)

Get married.   OK, I'm being flippant. But people who are happily married are less stressed than any other group. (Women who are unhappily married are among the most stressed.) Put time and effort into your relationship. Don't take it for granted or put it to the side while you concentrate on your children or your career. Your job doesn't reduce stress, and neither do your children. If you want to stress-proof your life, you need love.

Buy a pet.   Countless studies have discovered that having a cat or dog or other furry, friendly animal in your life can cause stress levels to plummet. One study even claims that cats purr on a frequency that is particularly de-stressing for humans. If love is lacking in your life from other sources or is disappointing, get a dog or cat.

"Success is about being able to extend love to people. Not in a big capital letter sense but in the every day—little by little, task by task, gesture by gesture, word by word."
RALPH FIENNES, actor

Defining idea...

How did it go?

Q I am very lonely. I don't have anyone to love me. What can I do?

A Well, I'm assuming you are doing all you can to combat this situation. Being lonely isn't good for your stress levels. In the meantime, use the power of touch to help you de-stress. Touch is one of the reasons close relationships are so beneficial and if you can't get it for free, there's nothing wrong with paying for it. Calm down. No, I don't mean that—but book a regular massage from a good therapist (emphasis on the good). It's not just the muscle relaxation that will de-stress you. Facials are good, too.

Q. I am really busy. I don't have time to reach out. Any suggestions?

A All you need to do to begin with is find 15 minutes a day to talk to your partner and 10 minutes a day to talk to a friend by phone. Start small. Get up early and have a cup of coffee with your partner if you simply don't have any other time. Or go to bed 15 minutes earlier—together, of course—and talk then. Reconnect. And then write in your planner the name of a friend or family member who is on your conscience—one for every night of the week. Call them. It doesn't need to be for long. Note: Texting or emailing don't count—they're fine methods for passing on train times but they are not a replacement for human contact.

49

Supplementary benefits

Managing stress is simply a matter of managing your body's chemistry. There is a whole battery of supplements that can help you do this.

They can give much needed support to help your body fight off the worst ravages of stress when the going gets tough.

If your diet is absolutely perfect then you might not need a vitamin and mineral supplement—but I doubt it. Food just ain't what it used to be and some people believe that our soil is not producing food with the same high nutrient content that our grandparents enjoyed. Even if you eat the sort of exemplary diet full of whole foods and never touch processed garbage, we face more stressful lives than our forebears—and stress "eats" up the body's nutrients. Those who have recently been ill, those who have undergone surgery, those who smoke, drink alcohol, or regularly run for a bus (suffer any regular stress, in other words), will all probably benefit from taking a good-quality multivitamin. All of these situations stress the body, and when the body's stressed it rips through vitamins and minerals.

But there are special occasions when extra help could be useful.

Here's an idea for you...

Zinc is very good for combating the effects of stress. Look for a supplement that combines zinc with the main antioxidant vitamins A, C, and E. This is a good one to reach for when you're really up against it.

If you have had a shock, or know that you are about to go through a stressful period—getting married, finals—think about investing in a B-complex supplement. This supports the nervous system. Your body can't store B vitamins and has to replace them every day (which is also the reason you won't overdose on them, though of course you should follow the instructions on the bottle).

Stress affects your immune system and if you seem to be getting every bug going, you will probably benefit from an antioxidant supplement. Vitamin C is a powerful antioxidant that has been shown to help the body recover from shock faster. (When patients were given antioxidant vitamins following trauma or surgery the mortality rate was 44 percent lower amongst them one month later than in a group of patients not given antioxidants.) Consider taking a vitamin C supplement two or three times a day. Around 500–1,000 mg in total should be enough. Don't take vitamin C if you have a history of kidney stones.

HERBAL HEALERS

Your pharmacist or local health food store can give you information on herbal supplements that help when you're stressed. Always talk to your pharmacist before buying herbal supplements. Some interfere with prescription drugs. When it comes to herbal help, the best supplement to reach for is ginseng. It is one of the herbs that Russian

Defining idea...

"The superior man is satisfied and composed. The mean man is always full of distress."
CONFUCIUS

scientists first dubbed the adaptogens—
"substances designed to put the organism into
a state of non-specific, heightened response in
order to better resist stresses and adapt to
extraordinary challenges." In other words, it
helps boost performance, which is why athletes
take it in the buildup to a big competition, as it
helps prime the body to operate at its peak in
stressful (especially competitive) situations.

Turn to IDEA 20, *Eat the stress-free way*, on food combining. This will give you a blueprint for healthy eating that will stand you in good stead when you want to improve your general nutrition.

Try another idea...

How *ginseng* works is still unknown. It's thought it might affect the part of the
brain called the hypothalamus, which controls the adrenal glands. By supporting
the adrenals, it reduces the amount of stress hormones produced. Thus, ginseng
minimizes the effects of stress on your body. Herbalists recommend you take
ginseng for no longer than three weeks without a break, as it loses its effectiveness
over time, but there are formulations that are designed to be taken all year round
that clinical research has shown do some good in defusing stress and boosting
energy. Ask your pharmacist for guidance.

Finally, there's another herb called *rhodiola* that is very good for helping you gain
focus and concentration under stressful conditions. Students who took the herb for
20 days outperformed those taking a placebo,
were less tired, and felt less stressed. You can
buy it in supplement form fairly easily now, and
like ginseng, if at all possible, start taking it a
couple of weeks before a stressful period.

"I honestly think you ought to calm down; take a stress pill, and think things over."
HAL, *2001: A SPACE ODYSSEY*

Defining idea...

How did it go?

Q   Stress is affecting my sleep. Are there any supplements that can help?

A   *Passiflora and valerian have been used for millennia to sedate naturally and defuse stress. They are particularly useful to help you sleep. You can buy tablet formulations that contain these herbs at pharmacies. A simple cup of chamomile tea before bed will help you sleep.*

Q   Isn't echinacea the best supplement to take to boost the immune system?

A   *Echinacea is good and I personally take it, but many of the echinacea supplements aren't of good quality so make sure you buy a reputable brand. Another herb that's just as good, and maybe better, is astragalus. Astragalus causes the release of interferon, the antiviral protein that helps fight off illness. If you are prone to stress-induced colds and flu, think of taking astragalus along with vitamin C.*

50

Burned out?

What is burnout? It's when a relationship—either work or personal—has gotten so bad that you just can't stand it any longer.

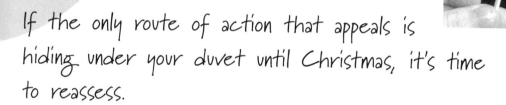

If the only route of action that appeals is hiding under your duvet until Christmas, it's time to reassess.

You're stressed. But just how stressed? Here are a few statements worth answering.

	Score
You fantasize a lot about your perfect life that doesn't include your dull/annoying partner/job	+1
You say "I can't take it anymore" at least once a week	+2
You feel unappreciated	+3
Tension is beginning to affect your health	+3
You wake up dreading the day ahead	+3
All you want to do in the evening is slump in front of the TV and sleep	+1

Score

4 or under = Mild level of dissatisfaction. This indicates that the present situation is stressful but potentially salvageable.

9 or under = Life is not good and you know you need to act.

10 or over = Burnout is imminent.

Here's an idea for you... **Spend 10 minutes every evening planning your next day. It's proven that you get one-fifth more work done if you review what you want to accomplish the next day in advance. Plus what you do achieve will likely be of higher quality.**

Dr. Dina Glouberman, who has written on the subject of burnout, defined it as what happens when "The love or meaning in what we are doing goes, but attachment drives us to carry on."

It's this attachment that you need to question. It's clear that some situations are easier to leave than others but if you have tried all you can to fix your particular hell and nothing improves, it's time to admit the unhappiness to yourself and others and move on. In our competitive world, it's hard to say "I may have made a mistake." The more time you've invested in the wrong life, the harder it is to give up on it. But the first step is simply admitting to yourself and perhaps a few trusted compadres that yes, you are human, you made a mistake.

There's nothing wrong with being unhappy with your life. See it as a positive. What it signals is that you have outgrown your present situation and that it's time to move on. Otherwise, the stress of living a life that isn't yours can be fearsome. You risk burnout—a state of collapse where you lose all joy in life. Your body gives out and your spirit gives up. It is extremely painful and can take months, even years, to come back from.

But even if you do burn out, it's not an unmitigated catastrophe either. For many it's the beginning of a new, more enlightened life. After spending their time in the metaphorical wilderness, they rethink their life and choose a new route.

Here's an exercise to help you get the process started:

■ Lie down. Breathe deeply. When you're calm, ask yourself "If I woke up and all my problems and worries had gone, how would I know a miracle had happened?"

■ How would you behave, talk, walk, think, if the miracle had happened?

■ How do you think your family and friends would know a miracle had happened?

■ If you were to assess your life right now somewhere between 0 and 10, with 0 being your worst life and 10 a full-scale miracle life, where would this day be on the scale?

■ What would need to happen for you to move one step up?

■ How would other people know that you had moved one step up?

This exercise helps you realize that it's not so much miracles (externals) that determine your happiness, but your behavior. You are in control.

Just about the best thing you can do right now is to build perfect moments into your life. IDEA 43, *Perfect moments*, will show you how.

Try another idea...

"Stress is an ignorant state. It believes that everything is an emergency."
O MAGAZINE

Defining idea...

How did it go?

Q   I know I have to look at the big picture but right now I just want to get to the weekend. Any ideas?

A   *Become more decisive. When you're stressed, what you've got to remember is that your body wants a decision—any decision—mucho pronto. Fight or flight is the classic decision and all your body craves is just that sort of black-and-white response. Make a decision. Any decision. And if you simply can't, then remember that NO decision is still a decision of sorts. Determine a time when you are going to think about what's stressing you. Decide definitely not to think about it any more until then and get on with your day as far as possible. Do your very best to banish dithering from your repertoire in every aspect from ordering a sandwich to making an important decision. Making fast decisions—bang, bang, bang—actually reduces stress.*

Q   Is it necessary to question myself so much?

A   *What I'm advocating is a form of therapy called solution therapy. It doesn't dwell on your problems or past but on how you can change your life step by step. If you are at the end of your tether, here's a very easy idea that can be summarized in five words: Don't let life just happen. Quite simply, you have to feel that you are back in control. Even if it's just of one small piece of your life. Start planning your escape—even if it's just for five minutes a day. It's been proven many times that those who write down long-term goals and then work backward, breaking those goals down into short-term aims, are almost certainly going to be happier—and richer—than those who drift through. You gotta have a plan.*

51

Run away, run away

Or to give it the grown-up name, retreat.

Some time alone with your own thoughts is deeply relaxing.

This idea is about obliterating the low-grade noise pollution that is now the background for most of our lives. Stop for a moment and think just how much noise is generated in your home now compared to the home you grew up in. Televisions in every room. Telephones wherever you go. Music playing where it never played before (in the workplace, on the end of the phone while you wait).

This constant barrage of noise is stressful. Here is a three-step plan to give yourself a break.

Step 1: Turn off the TV

TV will eat up your life. Some nine-year-olds are watching up to four hours a day and these children perform worse on all measures of intelligence and achievement. TV does exactly the same thing to adults. It is such a very passive form of entertainment—it's been proven that just lying on the couch doing nothing burns off more calories than watching TV, presumably because without TV at least you're generating some thoughts in your head. Reclaim hours of your time by limiting TV to one or two favorite programs a week. The rest of the time, turn it off. Listen to talk radio or music if you must have some noise.

Here's an idea for you...

Listen to some Bach, Chopin, or Beethoven prior to falling asleep. It's been shown that people who listen to classical music in bed fall asleep more easily and sleep better than people who watch TV or listen to other kinds of music.

Step 2: Be silent

This is difficult to manage if you live with other people. But take a day off work and experiment with no noise. No TV, no radio, no phone—switch them off. Silence is golden, honest. Not talking gives you the chance to listen to what your inner voice is trying to say to you.

Step 3: Retreat

The best way of doing this is to go on a dedicated retreat—all sort of institutions, religious or otherwise, run them. You can retreat and do yoga or dance or write or paint—or do absolutely nothing.

Of course, you don't have to leave home for that. It's much easier if you can escape but it's not impossible to put aside the hassles of everyday life and retreat in your own home. Clear away any clutter. Put away laptops, phones, planners, PDAs—all work paraphernalia should be banished. Make your house as calm, restful, and serene as possible.

SEVEN STEPS TO RETREATING

1. Set aside at least twenty-four hours, preferably longer. Warn everyone you know that you don't want to be disturbed.

2. If you have family, do the best you can to escape. One way of doing it is to come back on your own a day early from a break, or leave a day after everyone else.

3. Get in all the food you'll need. Plan ahead. Make it especially tasty and nutritious. You don't want to have to venture out for supplies.

4. Switch off the phone. Don't open your mail.

5. Don't speak.

6. This is your opportunity to go inward and not only relax fully but figure out what you really want to do with your life. For that reason keep the TV and radio off. Listen to music if you like but make it classical and not too emotional. Limit reading to an hour a day.

7. Write in a journal, paint or draw, invent recipes. Do anything creative.

Better yet, be very still. Lie on the couch with a blanket and your thoughts. Breathe. Stay silent for as long as you can.

The bath ritual described in IDEA 28, *Turning Japanese*, fits perfectly into a retreat.

Try another idea...

"Silence propagates itself and the longer talk has been suspended, the more difficult it is to find anything to say."
SAMUEL JOHNSON

Defining idea...

How did it go?

Q **Why can't I read as much as I want to?**

A *If you do, you'll benefit from resting from your usual routine but you won't get the full benefits. Many of us work really hard at not thinking too deeply by immersing ourselves in activities. Reading is just another activity that you can escape into. Food can be another, which is why there's the emphasis on planning healthy, delicious meals. Otherwise there's the temptation for some people to block emotions and thoughts with comfort foods—chocolate, alcohol, bread—just as others would use reading to the same ends.*

Q **I'm really resistant to the idea of a retreat. Isn't it just self-indulgent and a lot of fuss for nothing?**

A *There's no knowing what you'll find on a retreat, and there aren't any guarantees, but the fact that you are so resistant surely tells you there might be something you're trying to get away from. It's extraordinarily difficult for some people to set aside time to do nothing except indulge themselves—there are probably pretty good reasons for your resistance and you probably know what they are, which is why you don't want to be doing it. But if you're still in the dark, retreating is a great opportunity to listen to your own thoughts. That can be embarrassing. Your thoughts may strike you as pretty banal. Stick with it. Be aware of your body, where you are holding tension. The same applies to your mind. The point of creativity is that it helps you access thoughts that have been lurking in your subconscious. If you spend enough time quietly, eventually these thoughts will get the chance to surface.*

Make life easy

Give up coffee, don't smoke, get exercise—we're always being told that if we don't our stress will become worse. And you know what? It's true.

Wouldn't it be great if it was all a big, fat lie?

But, sorry, no. I'd love to tell you that it was, but I can't. Without a doubt, one of the main reasons our bodies and minds are buckling under stress is that our lifestyles are about as far removed from stress relieving as it's possible to be.

How do you fare? Answer these questions:

	Agree	Sometimes	Disagree
I'm happy with my body and I exercise regularly.	☐	☐	☐
When I suffer from stress I take steps to relax right away.	☐	☐	☐
I get enough sleep.	☐	☐	☐
I have a balanced diet.	☐	☐	☐
I don't drink more than one cup of tea or coffee a day.	☐	☐	☐
I plan regular weekends and vacations away.	☐	☐	☐
I don't overindulge in anything bad for me—nicotine, alcohol, or drugs.	☐	☐	☐
I have enough energy to do everything demanded of me.	☐	☐	☐

Here's an idea for you... **Start your day with oatmeal: The best stress-busting breakfast is a bowl of the stuff. If you can throw in some yogurt or milk (for their stress-reducing nutrients) even better. Oats have been shown to keep stress levels lower throughout the day than other breakfasts and although muesli made with oats is good, cooking the oats works best.**

Score 3 for an "agree," 2 for a "sometimes," and 1 for a "disagree."

If you score 12 or under, you need this idea more than most. If you scored between 12 and 20, your habits could still do with some fine-tuning.

Don't think about giving stuff up—take the attitude that you are adding good habits in. Follow each of these suggestions for a week or so, and when it's second nature add another.

Week 1

Drink a glass of water with every meal and every time you visit the bathroom.

Self-explanatory. Just do it. There are lots of smart alecks who will tell you we don't really need all that water. But water is almost unique in being a substance with no downside. Drinking water means you're not drinking something else that is probably bad for you. It also gives you more energy, and that's got to reduce your stress levels.

Week 2

Swap one of your regular cups of caffeine for one healthy cup. Caffeine stimulates the adrenal glands to work overtime. It's been found that four or five cups of coffee a day raises stress levels by a third. Living on the adrenaline produced by tea, coffee, fizzy drinks, and chocolate is just plain crazy. I know. I did it for years. Through my twenties I drank around four pints of espresso a day, no lie. Believe it or not, I slept like a log. But I was jittery and had little focus when I was awake. In South Africa, I discovered rooibus tea, now easily available as redbush tea. Unlike normal tea it is good for you, full of antioxidants but no caffeine. Unlike herbal tea, it tastes nice. Aim for no more than one cup of caffeine a day.

Along with these lifestyle changes, you need to relax regularly. Turn to IDEA 47, *Cherish yourself.*

Try another idea...

"In all affairs it's healthy now and then to hang a question mark on the things you have been taking for granted."
BERTRAND RUSSELL

Defining idea...

Week 3

Eat breakfast every single day. Studies show people who eat breakfast are more productive—and slimmer, incidentally—than those who miss it. I am not a breakfast person but, again, for the good of my health I forced myself to start eating within the first hour of waking up. This produces a huge difference in my concentration. Now I wouldn't miss it because I know myself the quality of my work is so much better.

Week 4

Every day eat...

One orange for vitamin C (or another helping of vitamin-C-rich food).

One helping of oats, fish, meat, or eggs (for vitamin B, necessary for beating stress).

One helping of broccoli or one helping of carrots, just great for antioxidants.

At lunch. One small serving of good-quality carbohydrate. Too much and you'll feel sleepy but one slice of whole grain bread or a fist-sized portion of whole grain pasta or rice will release the feel-good hormone serotonin.

Two to three servings of reduced-fat dairy, which is rich in natural opiates called casomorphins (have one serving with your evening meal if you have trouble sleeping).

At dinner. One small portion of good-quality protein (releases tryptophan which helps serotonin release).

This won't supply all the nutrients you need but it's a good start and it specifically delivers the nutrients you need to stay stress-free.

Week 5

Exercise. It is the single best thing you can do to reduce your stress levels and the best thing you can do for your complete health (with the exception of giving up smoking). Aerobic exercise (walking briskly, running, swimming) burns off excess stress hormones. Yoga lowers blood pressure in a matter of minutes, and after half an hour, stress levels have dropped dramatically.

Q **But doesn't exercise act as just another stressor on the body?**

How did it go?

A *Yes, but it's the kind of stress your body loves. And it's specifically what your body craves in response to stress. Here's a fact well worth remembering: The stress response is designed to run on a very short timescale. Adrenaline is released, you get the boost of adrenaline to help you solve a problem fast, finish the task at hand, and then move along to the relaxation part of the equation. So when you are in a stressful situation, the best thing you can do is move your body right away. A brisk walk around the block as fast as you can for 10 minutes is what you need rather than a trip to the bar. It makes sense that if your body is in one stressful situation after another you should take steps to regularly burn off excess stress hormones.*

Q **I'm a coffee addict. I hate herbal teas. What can I drink?**

A *Try decaf. Keep experimenting. Vitamin C helps withdrawal symptoms in heroin addicts—it might help you cut down on coffee. Vitamin C has another advantage: It jolts the brain into action, just like coffee, but without the jitteriness. Instead of the cups of coffee you use to get you through the day, eat vitamin-C-rich foods or take a vitamin C supplement.*

Bonus ideas

1

Manage your debt

I suspect we've all been there. Don't despair. Here are some positive techniques for getting out of debt.

Do you ever sit alone at night by the fire with your head in your hands and think, God have mercy on my soul, I have spawned a monster?

Although "spawning a monster" may be putting it a little too strongly, it would be nice to think that the banks, credit unions, and credit card providers who have fueled the current spending binge are suffering at least one or two pangs of guilt.

Many of us have been making the most of historically low interest rates to borrow money and to rack up debt on our credit cards. Our level of collective debt is unprecedented. It's estimated that around an average 12 percent of our income is eaten up by servicing debts.

Here's an idea for you... **This is strong medicine but if you're not convinced that you have a problem, try producing a consolidated debt statement. Every three months, compile details of all the money you owe anybody, including credit card debt, the outstanding balance on any loans you have, overdrafts, even the tenner you owe your best friend. This will give you an all too clear picture of the state of your finances.**

Defining idea...

"Anyone who lives within their means suffers from a lack of imagination."
OSCAR WILDE

And that figure is based on current interest rate levels. How would we cope if our bills suddenly went up by 20 percent? It only takes interest rates to rise a few percentage points and it could happen.

Part of the trouble is that the older of us have forgotten the years of double-digit rates, and the younger of us have no real experience of the cost of borrowing rearing up. OK, we can go on about how the credit card providers should be more responsible about unsecured lending. We can criticize them for setting low minimum repayments that can tempt customers to repay little more than the interest on the amount owed and so never pay off the debt. Ultimately, though, we are the ones who have to dig our way out of the debt hole. Waiting for a lottery win, or for a bequest from a distant relative, is no strategy.

TECHNIQUES FOR GETTING OUT OF DEBT

- **Stop the rot.** If you have multiple credit cards, identify which one has the most draconian interest rate and shred it. Don't tuck it in a drawer and rely on your willpower not to use it. History suggests this is not a great tactic. If you can, consider transferring the debt on this card to the one carrying the least interest.

- **Talk to your creditors.** Let them know you're having problems. Depending on the extent of your debt, you may want to agree to a strategy for clearing the debt. Figure out how much you can realistically afford to pay. Focus on the most important monthly payment—mortgage/rent, gas, electricity, etc.

- **Don't panic but don't ignore the problem.** You may have seen nature programs where creatures stay very, very still in order to evade predators. Your debt won't go away; in fact, ignoring it guarantees that it will get worse as the interest builds up and your creditors start to hound you. Don't ignore court papers.

- **Don't pay for advice.** There are plenty of sources of free help and counseling. Talk to your bank, ask your employer for advice, check the Federal Trade Commission's website.

Getting into severe debt is horrible—I know, I've been there (it happens when you write for a living!). The crucial first step back to solvency is to face up to the fact that you're in debt and to recognize that you need to adopt a conscious strategy to get out of it.

"I can get no remedy against this consumption of the purse: Borrowing only lingers and lingers it out, but the disease is incurable."
WILLIAM SHAKESPEARE

Defining idea...

239

How did it go?

Q **It seems like every morning I get junk mail suggesting that I could save money by consolidating all my debts. Is this worthwhile?**

A *Please be wary of consolidation loans. The problem is that these loans often have to be secured against your home, and there is a real risk of losing the roof over your head if there is any lapse in your ability to pay off the amount. A consolidation loan also manages to turn what could be a relatively short-term debt into a long-term financial commitment.*

Q **Even so, surely it's worth trying if you're repaying at a lower interest rate?**

A *Only if you are incredibly self-disciplined about it. There's a real danger that having used the loan to clear your credit cards, you start to reapply debt to your credit card and end up with a double debt whammy of having to simultaneously pay the consolidation loan and whatever you are building up on your credit card. In my book, taking out a consolidation loan has to go hand in hand with shredding your credit card.*

This idea originally appeared in *Detox Your Finances: Earn More, Spend Less, and Make Your Money Work as Hard as You Do*, by John Middleton.

2

Reality check

Live to work—or work to live? Think carefully about your work–life balance or you may find yourself stuck on the work treadmill until life passes you by completely.

You work late, arriving home just in time to see your children as they go to bed if you're lucky. You eat, do household chores, and go to bed. In the morning, you get up and start all over again. Surely there must be a better way to live.

Do you feel that you are struggling to find meaning in your life? Feel as though you're in a spiritual and emotional vacuum; or that you're dislocated from anything "real"? Perhaps you try to fill the void with "things." You go on recreational shopping trips for new, meaningless trinkets until you are trapped by an ever-growing pile of *stuff*. It may be attractive, and no doubt it's expensive, but it conspires to weigh you down. Acquiring more stuff becomes an obsession—or an addiction. Each boost gives you a high, but it is fleeting and soon needs replenishing.

Here's an idea for you...

If you're thinking of downshifting, make a list of the pros and cons. This might sound like the old-fashioned advice your mom used to give you, but it works. Dare to daydream. Create the picture of how you want your life to be. Once you have this in your mind, craft your list of pros—more time with the children, less stress, no commuting, being more self-sufficient. But consider the cons, too. Will you be able to cope with isolation, hard work, harsh weather, and surviving on a reduced income? Read as many personal accounts of downshifting as possible so you get a realistic picture of the bliss—and agony—you may experience.

TOO MUCH STUFF—NOT ENOUGH TIME!

You gather wealth and possessions to gain kudos. The amount of expensive *stuff* we have is a measure of our success. But there's a nagging feeling in the back of your mind: Although you are resources rich, you are time poor. You spend your money on buying back time—paying other people to care for your children, clean your home, do your ironing. Your mind races constantly, so you pay for relaxation and exercise—going to the spa, the gym, and the massage therapist.

Increasing numbers of people are now refusing to be a part of this "stress and spend" lifestyle. In Europe alone, 12 million people have decided to downshift. That may mean moving to a less stressful—and potentially lower income—job and moving to a smaller, less expensive house. At the other end of the scale it may mean moving to a place in the country and living a more self-sufficient lifestyle. Whatever form of downshifting you decide to experience, you must ensure you are fully prepared for a major lifestyle change.

You may be excited by the idea of living a more simple life and working for yourself, either setting up your own business or doing freelance work for other companies. You may also yearn to spend more time outdoors, with your hands in the soil growing your own food and collecting eggs from your warm, fluffy chickens.

LOOK BEFORE YOU LEAP

What you don't want to do is leap in, feetfirst, and have to crawl ignominiously back to city life in a year's time—as many people do. They did the dreaming, but forgot to take a cold, hard look at the challenges they would face. Can you face the isolation—either the type that can come with rural life, or the type that can come with working from home? If you hope to spend lots of time outside, are you prepared for bitter cold? It's not always sunny and idyllic, you know.

Your baseline at all times should be the answer to this question: What gives you joy? Then take steps to include it in your life.

"Downshifting isn't just about getting away from what you don't want; it's also about moving toward what you really want to do."
NICK WILLIAMS, author of The Work We Were Born To Do

Defining idea...

243

How did it go?

Q **I've always wanted to run a small farm, but the more I read, the more scared I get about the amount of grueling, messy work involved. Do these reservations mean my dream will wither and never come true?**

A *It's wise to be cautious. I've lost count of the bitterly cold days when I've dreaded the chores facing me. But I wouldn't swap my life for anything—organic veggies on my doorstep and startled deer staring at me as the mist clears in the early morning. The key is to check out what you can cope with. Stay at a farmhouse for a break and see what work is involved. Read, read, and read some more—books, websites, online communities—to get as full and real a picture as possible. You may still want a farm or you could decide to compromise and move to a more rural area with a large garden for vegetables and a few hens. Just make sure you make the right choice for you and your dream will blossom.*

Q **Can you really live a self-sufficient life without moving to the country? I'd like to downshift, but I don't really want to move away from my house in the suburbs.**

A *It is possible to downshift to an extent without moving. For example, look at your outgoing expenses—where can you make savings that will enable you to work fewer hours? How large is your garden? You can grow a wide variety of crops in an amazingly small space. Do your homework and you should be able to make real changes in your situation.*

This idea originally appeared in *Downshift to the Good Life: Scale It Down and Live It Up*, by Lynn Huggins-Cooper.

3

Stress reaction

You can't avoid the taxman; neither can you avoid getting older. You can, however, avoid the stress that may contribute to getting your blood pressure up and bringing you down. Here's how.

You're on your way to work, driving along your usual route. As always you reach a certain point and traffic starts to slow. Before long you are stationary.

Just like you, the steering wheel is feeling the pressure as you grip it tighter. Your jaw muscles tense, reflecting how you feel. Inside you're getting ready to explode, and before long you'll be thumping the horn. It's hardly the way you should be in charge of a car, is it? You see, stress makes us adopt bad habits, and bad habits cause our blood pressure to rise.

If you stop banging your head against the wall, the headache will go away. It's simple advice, but it's true. Likewise, if you choose another route, or another method of traveling to work—perhaps travel at a different time—your journey will be an easier, more relaxed one.

Here's an idea for you...

Take a moment to think about what causes you stress on a regular basis. Perhaps it's people trying to sell you stuff over the phone, or the fact that there's never milk in the fridge at work. Now make the necessary change so that you solve the problem and avoid the stress.

Many stresses in our life are avoidable. It doesn't have to be a case of "same shit, different day." We know these stresses exist because they make us angry, irritable, fed-up on a regular, even daily, basis. They are the hurdles that get in the way of our day running smoothly. The colleague who constantly interrupts you while you're trying to work. The fact that every morning there's always a line at the train station ticket office that on more than one occasion has meant you have actually missed or come close to missing your train. These are all predictable stresses. They are also minor things that shouldn't cause the trouble they do. But the fact that they keep happening means that, left unaddressed, they assume huge proportions. The fact that they are predictable is good, because you can do something about them.

If you play golf and you keep slicing your shot, you change your grip and you overcome the problem. If your cooking doesn't come out quite right, you alter the ingredients. The change is only a small one, but it can make all the difference.

A gentle word in your colleague's ear explaining that you have something important to complete and need to concentrate. Buying a ticket the day before or even getting a pass so you only have to line up once a week or once a month means you avoid the stress. These are simple steps, which don't take much effort, but can bring you closer to the stress-free environment you crave.

The reason many of us just put up with the stress and suffer unnecessarily is that we either believe we have no alternative or we think it'll take too much effort to change the way we behave. How many times have you said, "Oh there's nothing I can do about it. I guess I'll just have to live with it"? Even though you may feel comfortable doing what you are doing, it's going to be causing you problems.

Nowadays piles of paperwork are a major source of stress. These paper mountains spring up without permission. You may not be able to brush these under the carpet, but you can hide them. Not so that you forget about them, because that can cause some serious stress, believe me. But out of sight is out of mind. I know someone who had his computer in his bedroom, surrounded by piles of work-related papers. It was the last thing he saw before turning off the light and going to sleep, and the first thing he saw when he woke up. It stressed him out to no end. But he solved the problem, he simply moved the computer and the paperwork to another room, leaving the bedroom for what it's supposed to be for: relaxation, sleep, and, of course, sex.

> "He who rejects change is the architect of decay. The only human institution which rejects progress is the cemetery."
> HAROLD WILSON

Defining idea...

247

How did it go? **Q** **My colleague still interrupts me even after I've told her I'm busy. Can you save her from a bloody and imminent death?**

A *There are a number of ways to address this problem. If your colleague is disturbing you with non-work things, you could say that you are too busy to chat at the moment and that you'd like to catch up over coffee a little later. If it's work-related things, then ask her to list them and set a time when you can talk through them. Door open and door closed is a method of communication some people use to overcome this problem—always make sure that your colleagues understand what this means. Sometimes you just have to be firm and direct and say that you do not want to be disturbed unless it's an emergency. If you're anxious about addressing your colleague, rehearse what you are going to say first to build up your confidence.*

Q **I know if I put things out of sight I'll forget to do them. Any suggestions?**

A *Try creating a "things to do box." This way you will know where the things are that need doing, but you will not be constantly seeing how large the pile is. You'll be less stressed this way since often it's being reminded about it, particularly when you are doing something else, which causes more stress than the amount of stuff that needs your attention. By being in control and it being your choice when you look at the pile of work, the stress will not be so great.*

This idea originally appeared in *Control Your Blood Pressure: Smart Ways to Get Healthy Where It Counts Most,* by Dr. Rob Hicks.

Where it's at...

52 Brilliant Ideas

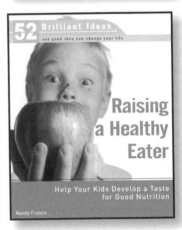

UNLEASH YOUR CREATIVITY
978-0-399-53325-9

LIVE LONGER
978-0-399-53302-0

SECRETS OF WINE
978-0-399-53348-8

DETOX YOUR FINANCES
978-0-399-53301-3

CELLULITE SOLUTIONS
978-0-399-53326-6

RAISING A HEALTHY EATER
978-0-399-53339-6

PERIGEE An imprint of Penguin Group (USA)

one good idea can change your life

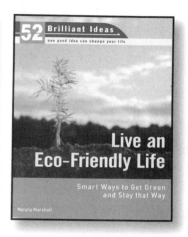

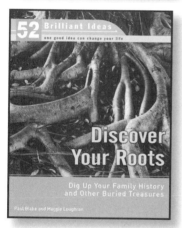

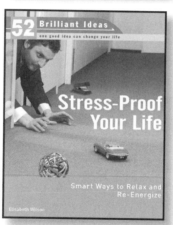

PUMP UP YOUR WORKOUT
978-0-399-53409-6

GREAT SEX
978-0-399-53392-1

LIVE AN ECO-FRIENDLY LIFE
978-0-399-53396-9

DISCOVER YOUR ROOTS
978-0-399-53322-8

STRESS-PROOF YOUR LIFE
978-0-399-53405-8

SLEEP DEEP
978-0-399-53323-5

Available wherever books are sold or at penguin.com